Praise for *Become Your Own Boss in 12 Months, Revised and Expanded*

"Best start-up book I ever read!"

—Alfred A. Edmond Jr., SVP/executive editor-at-large of Black Enterprise; "The Successpert"

"Pay attention to Melinda Emerson. She is smart, concise, and on-point all the time. In *Become Your Own Boss in 12 Months*, she provides great insight on things that are tough to navigate. She makes them easy to understand."

—Marcus Lemonis, CNBC's *The Profit*

"In *Become Your Own Boss in 12 Months*, Melinda Emerson has laid out a proven plan for business success. Follow her step-by-step guide to start your dream business."

—Jon Gordon, eleven-time bestselling author of *The Carpenter* and *The Power of Positive Leadership*

"With *Become Your Own Boss in 12 Months*, Melinda Emerson has created a comprehensive checklist for the first-time entrepreneur that is sure to save you thousands of dollars in lost time and lost revenue."

—Jay Samit, bestselling author of *Disrupt You!* and *Future Proofing You*

"This is a must-read for start-ups and existing entrepreneurs working through their digital pivot."

—Mike Michalowicz, author of *Profit First* and *Get Different*

Praise for *Become Your Own Boss in 12 Months, Revised and Expanded*

"This book provides a complete step-by-step approach to starting a successful business. Melinda Emerson doesn't leave anything out! You'll want to follow her prescriptive advice closely."

—Steve Strauss, *USA TODAY* small business columnist

"*Become Your Own Boss in 12 Months* has everything you need to launch or reinvent a small business. Melinda Emerson's unique approach provides a step-by-step guide to build the business of your dreams."

—Scott Jeffrey Miller, *Wall Street Journal* bestselling author of *Everyone Deserves a Great Manager*

"*Become Your Own Boss in 12 Months* is the book I wish I had when I decided to leave Corporate America and start my own business. Melinda Emerson helps entrepreneurs ask themselves the questions that will help them create the financial freedom they've been looking for."

—Minda Harts, bestselling author of *The Memo*

"Melinda Emerson has done it again! *Become Your Own Boss in 12 Months* is loaded with everything you need to know before you leave your 9 to 5 job behind and venture into business ownership. If you're ready to embrace the freedom of entrepreneurship, you need this excellent book!"

—Stephanie Chandler, author of *The Nonfiction Book Publishing Plan*

Praise for *Become Your Own Boss in 12 Months, Revised and Expanded*

"*Become Your Own Boss in 12 Months* is a must-read for anyone looking to launch a new e-commerce or service business. Melinda Emerson's step-by-step system will put you on the path to business success."

—John Jantsch, author of
Duct Tape Marketing and *The Ultimate Marketing Engine*

"Whether you are just getting started as an entrepreneur or you need a solid refresher to up your business game, *Become Your Own Boss in 12 Months* is the book for you. It's overflowing with the practical tips, advice, and specific action steps that will lead you from working for someone else to working for yourself. This is your time, and this book is the only guide you need!"

—Donna Maria Coles Johnson, president of Indie Business Network

"What impresses me about the book is the basic questions it guides the reader through—questions that enthusiastic new business owners fail to address until it is too late. Melinda Emerson knows what it takes to start a successful business!"

Barry Moltz, small business expert

"Whether you are getting ready to start a small business or looking for tips and information for building your existing brand and operating smarter, *Become Your Own Boss in 12 Months* will become your invaluable go-to resource."

—Rieva Lesonsky, small business expert; SmallBizDaily.com

Praise for *Become Your Own Boss in 12 Months, Revised and Expanded*

"The new content in *Become Your Own Boss in 12 Months* on how to sell and market online is exactly what is needed to help business owners get started with e-commerce. Melinda has the experience, wisdom, and skill to move you from wannabe entrepreneur to flourishing entrepreneur."

—Pamela Slim, author of *Body of Work*

"Melinda Emerson has poured more than twenty years of her experience into this step-by-step guide to business success. Read this book and then use the advice. You'll be glad you did."

—Ramon Ray, author of *The Celebrity CEO*

"Melinda Emerson has poured her everything into this book. With more than twenty years of experience, her step-by-step guide to business success is both timeless and timely. Read this book, and then immediately use the wisdom, knowledge, and understanding to build your business. This book is just that darn good!"

—John Lawson, e-commerce business expert

"Melinda Emerson is the number one expert you need to follow if you're stepping into business ownership. Don't even think about going into business without reading this book. A step-by-step road map for success, *Become Your Own Boss in 12 Months* presents time-tested wisdom, thoughtful development, and strategic marketing know-how to convert any dreamer into a successful business owner."

—Amy Franko, author of *The Modern Seller*

BECOME YOUR OWN BOSS IN 12 MONTHS

REVISED AND EXPANDED

A Month-by-Month Guide to a Business That *Works* Today!

MELINDA EMERSON, MBA

Adams Media

New York London Toronto Sydney New Delhi

For my JoJo. Being your mom is my heart's joy.
I can't wait to see the places you will go.

Adams Media
An Imprint of Simon & Schuster, Inc.
100 Technology Center Drive
Stoughton, Massachusetts 02072

Copyright © 2021 by Melinda Emerson.

All rights reserved, including the right to reproduce this book or portions thereof in any form whatsoever. For information address Adams Media Subsidiary Rights Department, 1230 Avenue of the Americas, New York, NY 10020.

This Adams Media trade paperback edition September 2021

ADAMS MEDIA and colophon are trademarks of Simon & Schuster.

For information about special discounts for bulk purchases, please contact Simon & Schuster Special Sales at 1-866-506-1949 or business@simonandschuster.com.

The Simon & Schuster Speakers Bureau can bring authors to your live event. For more information or to book an event contact the Simon & Schuster Speakers Bureau at 1-866-248-3049 or visit our website at www.simonspeakers.com.

Interior image © 123RF/allegro7

Manufactured in the United States of America

1 2021

Library of Congress Cataloging-in-Publication Data
Names: Emerson, Melinda F., author.
Title: Become your own boss in 12 months / Melinda Emerson, MBA.
Description: Revised and Expanded Edition. | Stoughton, MA: Adams Media, 2021. | Revised edition of the author's Become your own boss in 12 months, 2015.
Identifiers: LCCN 2021018947 | ISBN 9781507215982 (pb) | ISBN 9781507215999 (ebook)
Subjects: LCSH: Self-employed. | New business enterprises--Management.
Classification: LCC HD8036 .E49 2021 | DDC 658.1/1--dc23
LC record available at https://lccn.loc.gov/2021018947

ISBN 978-1-5072-1598-2
ISBN 978-1-5072-1599-9 (ebook)

CONTENTS

PART I—GET READY!   31

PART II—GET SET!   89

PART III—GO! 241

WHAT THIS BOOK CAN DO FOR YOU

In twelve months, you can be the owner of your own successful small business.

It could be anything from a company that creates website content for fashion companies to one that organizes scientific lab experiments for high schools. It could be based anywhere from Bangor, Maine, to Manilla, Philippines. It could sell to consumers or other businesses. But no matter where your customers or business is located, like most small businesses today, you will sell online, and there's a good chance you will be nimble and niche-oriented.

This book will show you how to achieve and surpass your goal of being a small business owner and will demonstrate that it's achievable in one year or less.

Here's how it works:

■ Twelve months out, you'll begin by creating a life plan—deciding whether you're really the kind of person who can run a small business.

- Eleven months out, you'll build a financial plan so you know where your launch money's going to come from and if you need to clean up your credit.
- Ten months out, you're ready to validate your business concepts and hire specialists: a CPA and a lawyer to help with your planning.
- Nine months out, it's time for you to identify your target customer and pull together your marketing plan and sales projections.
- Seven months out, it's getting close to launch time. This is when you'll pull together your website, which is your number one sales tool and formulate a plan for content and search engine optimization to put yourself in front of the largest number of potential customers.
- Six months out, you'll start working hard to establish a social media brand. Launch your website and begin assembling your employees. As you approach launch, you'll develop customer service systems that will keep your customers coming back and give you an edge over your competition.
- Finally, just weeks out, you'll do a final check: Is everything in place? Then you're ready to go.

Once you've hit the twelve-month mark and your business is up and running, you'll learn how to keep it going. It will take special skills to do this, since the business environment and marketing channels are constantly changing. More businesses are conducted online these days, and as the business owner you must learn online selling techniques. Customers expect personalization and performance, and they have so many choices. People are addicted to free shipping. And the speed of business keeps increasing. The good news is that amid all this change, the fundamentals of small businesses remain the same: The world is still waiting for solutions. You must have a good product, good processes, good pricing and a compelling offer. If you build something unique that solves a problem, it will sell, if you get the marketing right. What's key to succeeding in business is knowing the steps you must take to become a dynamic entrepreneur.

When I started my own business, I developed the twelve-month timeline you'll find in these pages. Throughout this book, you'll find examples—a lot of them—that I drew from my own experience: You'll see those comments as "Emerson's Essentials" and "Emerson's Experience." Everyone makes mistakes; I made some big ones, and I had to learn from them. *Become Your Own Boss in 12 Months, Revised and Expanded* shows you how to avoid these errors. And if problems develop along the way, this book gives you a set of solutions, embodied in the list of "Emerson's Action Steps" that close most chapters. The solutions are key to updating your business plan and keeping it current so you can deal with everyday issues as they arise.

Your thoughtful planning is the most important aspect of creating your own business in twelve months! A clear, developed plan and a schedule that you create and stick to will help you avoid a lot of pitfalls. As you study this book you'll learn what you do *not* know about running a business and develop a way to train yourself to become a successful entrepreneur. Remember, your business plan is your road map to success. Use it to design exactly what your business will be, what it will sell, and how it will attract and keep customers. Once you have those elements in place, you're ready to begin.

SMALL business resource

Use me as a resource beyond this book. I'm @SmallBizLady on all social sites, and my blog is https://succeedasyourownboss.com. I also offer a Become Your Own Boss course that will walk you step-by-step through the systems I teach in this book. All my online courses will solidify your foundation to develop a sustainable and profitable small business. For more information, head over to www.smallbizladyuniversity.com.

CHAPTER 1

So You Think You Want to Be an Entrepreneur

This is not a decision to take lightly. Becoming your own boss means not only having a solid business idea but also knowing the "business of running a business."

Many people think a small business starts with a business plan. That's part of it, of course, but there's more to it. Before you write a business plan, you must develop a life plan. You need to start a business that aligns with your personal and professional goals.

You must consider if you have the courage, persistence, confidence, skills, work ethic, and focus needed to succeed as your own boss. You need to know if you can handle all the jobs entrepreneurs must do. Unlike a regular employee of a business, your job will not be specialized. You'll be chief salesperson, secretary, payroll clerk, social media strategist, IT technician, and HR manager. Once you make a sale, you must service the customers.

You must focus on numbers and measurement. Too many small businesses operate at a net loss and do not realize this until it's too late. Use this book to reduce your learning curve.

Here are five questions every would-be entrepreneur should answer before going into business:

1. **How much does it cost to make your product or deliver your professional service?** Look at your hard costs, including labor, materials, packaging, and shipping. Factor in a percentage of your soft costs, such as marketing and your business support services.

2. **How much do you sell the product for?** Look at the competition and pull industry data to determine whether your cost plus a healthy profit margin is reasonable in the marketplace.

3. **Can your business be easily copied?** What is your secret sauce that only you bring to your business? If your business can be easily duplicated by bigger competitors, that is a sign that you might need to rethink it and come up with a unique twist.

4. **Does your marketing and branding make sense?** In order to connect with customers, you must have a good product or service, good pricing, a good offer, and good follow-up systems. Your customer engagement will define your brand. The name of your business should indicate what you do. Do you have a specific niche target customer for your product or service? Do you have a strong marketing message? Do you have a helpful website and a good shopping cart experience? Is your packaging attractive? Do you have a video marketing strategy? Do you have a monthly marketing budget to buy online ads?

5. **Can you sell yourself?** In business, you are selling yourself as much as you are selling your product or service. You must carry the confidence to make people believe in you and what you are selling.

If you become a parent, many people will tell you that the first five years are the toughest for parents. That little person is dependent on you from the moment of conception to the day you put him or her on the yellow cheese wagon headed for kindergarten. Your job isn't over once your child goes to school full time, but at that point children can do some things for themselves.

The same is true for a small business. If you think you work hard now, just wait until you become your own boss. You will come to know what the word "sacrifice" means. You'll scale back eating out, buying the latest gadget, and shopping whenever you feel like it. You'll cook at home and eliminate all unnecessary spending. Yes, that well-deserved surf and turf dinner at your favorite restaurant is now an unnecessary expense. Small businesses typically take eighteen to twenty-four months to break even and three years to generate any profits. Year four is when a business blossoms into a self-sustaining entity. It will take every bit of enthusiasm and energy you have to grow your business into a viable enterprise with a powerful social media brand.

Being a successful entrepreneur is also about having patience. You need to be patient with yourself, your employees, your strategic partners and, most importantly, your customers. Despite challenges, if you can just hold on, being an entrepreneur can be the most satisfying professional experience of your life.

So the first step is to decide whether you're cut out for the entrepreneur lifestyle.

The Entrepreneurial Mindset

The first step, they say, is always the hardest, and that's true in business. You must take a long, hard, honest look at yourself and decide if you're ready for the entrepreneurial lifestyle. Here are some things to consider:

Entrepreneurs are always thinking of new and better ways to do things. Do the following attributes describe you?

- You'd prefer to be in charge.
- You think your boss is generally clueless.
- You feel underused by your supervisors and dissatisfied with your job.
- You know you would do things differently if it were your company.
- You sit at your desk calculating the amount of money you make for your employer, thinking that you should be working for yourself.
- You are convinced that you could do a better job than the folks above you.

Entrepreneurs are natural leaders. They are self-motivated and creative thinkers. They can make a decision quickly and stick to it. Entrepreneurs are visionaries, hard workers, and extremely perceptive. They typically have demanding personalities and are extroverted. They are passionate risk takers who are always seeking to improve upon current conditions.

On the flip side, at times such people can be stubborn and impatient. Entrepreneurs are not always good listeners or coachable, and can be paranoid and territorial.

If any of this describes you, or if you possess any of these qualities, then entrepreneurship may be for you. But before you go into business, there are six things you must have:

1. A life plan
2. A solid business idea
3. Exceptional credit
4. A business plan
5. A supportive family or spouse
6. Faith

The Life of a Small Business Owner

Becoming your own boss means more than sacrifice. It means long, hard, consistent work, often with little reward up front. That's why you need a life plan before you commit to your own business. You need to evaluate what you want out of life first.

Consider the following questions:

- What kind of lifestyle do you want to have as an entrepreneur?
- How big do you want your business to get in terms of profits and staff?
- Will you have employees?
- How many hours a week will you work?
- Do you need to meet the school bus every day or take off every Friday?
- Are you willing to work seven days a week? For how many years can you keep that up?
- Will you need a partner, and could you handle working with one?
- How will you fund your household while you build your business?
- Are you fit to work from home?

You may have a great business idea, but you must decide if it's a good business for you and your family. Try this exercise: Close your eyes and think hard about what the best day in your business will look like five years from now. It may help if you write it down. Spend some time on it and get it fixed in your head.

Once you have that vision, consider what it will mean to you and to those you love for that day to become a reality. Be careful creating this vision. Make sure it includes personal and professional aspirations. Don't confuse success with happiness.

Your Business Idea

Even if you come to the conclusion that you can be an entrepreneur, you must decide if you should. In other words, do you have a solid business idea? On a sheet of paper, write down answers to the following questions:

- Who is your niche target customer?
- What problem are you solving for your customer?
- How much competition is there in your market?
- Does your business solve some unmet need?
- What will be your unique value proposition?
- Are you selling products or services or both?
- Will you sell wholesale, retail, e-commerce, private label, etc.?
- Will your business be bricks and mortar, online, or both?
- Will you need a manufacturing partner?

Researching the industry, the market opportunity, the potential customer, and the competition is crucial. Your research will also help determine whether there's a viable market for your product or service.

Know Your Business

Your business venture should be something in which you have experience or professional training. The only exception to this rule is if you buy into a franchise or take over an existing business. In those cases, the franchise company typically provides some training, or there are people working in the business who can help provide institutional information about it. (Even in those cases, don't buy a food franchise if you have never worked in a restaurant.) Work for a business like the one you want to start for at least a year before starting on your own. Do not start a daycare center if you have never worked with kids, just because you heard those kinds of businesses make a lot of money.

Love the Work

On those hard days when there's no money and plenty of work to do, your love for your business will be the only thing that keeps you going. Also, when you love what you do, your customers can see that, and they will be that much more interested in doing business with you. Savvy business owners figure out how to do something they are passionate about and get paid for it.

EMERSON'S experience

There is always something that inspires or drives someone to become an entrepreneur. In my case, after three TV news jobs, I decided I had to figure out another way to earn a living. My dream job was really a nightmare. Seven years earlier, as a sophomore in college, I had been inspired by Oprah Winfrey, who started Harpo Studios.

I decided that one day I would have my own production company.

When I started my business, I had no idea how to use a basic spreadsheet or presentation software. I barely knew Microsoft Word. One of my mentors let me call her administrative assistant and ask questions about how to format business letters, do mail merges, and such. I am sure I gave her headaches, but she graciously gave me the support I needed. I later invested in computer-based training to learn the software I would be using.

Consider Business Education

If you're in college and you think that you might want to start a business someday, double major or at least minor in business or marketing. If you are already interested in starting your own business, write an outline of your business ideas as soon as possible.

As a business owner, you must constantly look for ways to improve your skills. Start a library of books about small business, marketing, finance, sales, and leadership. In the Further Resources section at the end of this book, you'll find a list of the top small business books every entrepreneur should read. Use this list to gather even more information about running a successful business.

How Are Your People Skills?

Your ability to interact with people, including customers, staff, and strategic partners, will be critical to your business success. Many entrepreneurs get frustrated managing employees, even if they have management experience in a corporate setting. If you are a business owner who has never dealt with external customers or worked in a team environment, your people skills may need some polishing.

It all comes down to communication. Consider what you're trying to accomplish and do your best to determine what level of communication is required. It could be a face-to-face discussion, a memo, an email, a video chat, a handwritten note, or a phone call. Or you may need to use more than one method. Try to always end any interaction by recapping deliverables and any action items. Do not hesitate to follow up any communication in writing.

It's about the Money

There's no way around it: Starting a business is expensive. It will be a while before you see a return on your investment; you may go without a regular paycheck for years. That's why, before you hand the boss your walking papers and box up the personal things in your cubicle, you'd better make sure you and your family are on solid financial ground, and your business is making money consistently.

You'll need exceptional credit and a significant amount of savings— enough money to support yourself and your family for at least twelve to twenty-four months—along with the first year of working capital for your new business. Sometimes you can rely on your spouse's paycheck or a nest egg that you've saved and scrimped and scraped together. Whatever the case, it's essential that you start your business from a position of financial security. Otherwise, you could be finished before you have even started.

Build a Plan for Success

Once you complete your life plan and your financial inventory, and evaluate your business idea, you will know what you want out of life as an entrepreneur and whether you've got the resources to accomplish it. Draw on the research you've already done on your industry: Learn the trends and make sure you understand how big the potential market is for your product or service. After your personal path is clear, it's time to formulate your business model.

EMERSON'S essentials

Every small business needs a plan. You cannot be in business successfully without a business plan. Just as you would never take a trip without knowing how much money you were going to need for the whole vacation, how long it was going to take to get to your destination, and where you were going to stop overnight, you can't start a business without knowing how much it costs to be in business and the structure of how the business will operate.

Writing a business plan is not as hard as you may think. Go online to www.bplans.com to review hundreds of sample business plans and use business plan software such as www.liveplan.com to help you get your business going. Pace yourself. Work on your plan two hours a day. Make

21

time before work or after the kids go to bed. Plan to invest enough time to get it right.

After making a dent in your business plan with the software, take a business plan course from a nonprofit business training organization, Small Business Development Center (SBDC), Women's Business Development Center (WBDC), or a community college in your area. Remember: Until you have a complete business plan with financial projections, you are just a person with an idea. You are not in business! Tim Berry, noted business planning expert, says not having a business plan is like walking down a major city street with a blindfold on. Put yourself at an advantage by setting measurable goals and developing a budget for your business. You'll need a business plan to present to investors or a funder to secure a microloan. No one will loan you money for your idea without a business plan that has realistic financial projections.

EMERSON'S experience

I have rewritten my business plan every year that I have been in business. The third time I rewrote my business plan, I won a business plan competition in Philadelphia. The prize was $20,000 and free office space for a year.

Plans change once they're exposed to the market. In the first year or two of your business, you must revisit your business plan every three months or so to see what has changed. You'll need to update it to reflect the market conditions. Your business plan is a blueprint to help you stay on top of your business goals and sales projections.

A Supportive Family or Spouse

Business owners who are married can benefit from a spouse who supports the household financially and provides health benefits while the enterprise is getting off the ground. However, suddenly becoming a one-salary family is tricky. Make sure that your spouse is behind your decision. If not, your dream can turn into a nightmare. It is very hard to start a business. If you come home to negativity every night, your likelihood of success is that much tougher.

EMERSON essentials

An unsupportive spouse can kill a business faster than a bad marketing plan. So check in with that person to see if they are on board with your career change.

Treat your spouse, who is sacrificing alongside you, like your number one customer. Make sure there's good communication between you. Show appreciation for the partner who works 9 to 5. They will be doing most of the heavy lifting in the household, taking care of homework, dinner, and bed and bath for the kids, since your main focus will be this new business. Remember that eventually your spouse will want to see money coming in the door instead of going out. So you need a plan for success, and must share that plan.

You Gotta Have Faith

If your business is a recipe, faith is a key ingredient. Faith gives you the confidence to start your business and the courage to push forward. You will need your faith the most on those days when things do not work out. Your faith in your business will help you look for the lesson first and make it right with the client. You should work hard to keep your emotions in check when you or someone on your team makes an expensive mistake. Lick your wounds, but don't dwell on bad days—you'll need to fight on another day. Faith will help you set aside your ego and hire people smarter than you and trust them to do their jobs. Faith will help you stay honest with your vendors and customers. Religious or not, you can always pray for guidance.

Is Entrepreneurship for You?

Once you've read to this point, if your passion and commitment and faith are still strong…go for it! Your dream of entrepreneurship can be a reality!

CHAPTER 2

WHY DOES IT TAKE
TWELVE MONTHS?

Karen had a small business knitting custom scarves at her kitchen table. One day, a man at her doctor's office asked her about the lovely knit scarf she was wearing. She explained that she'd made it. The man's wife was a department store buyer, and he was looking for a unique gift for her birthday.

Karen knitted a special scarf for his wife. The woman liked it so much she wanted to stock it in her store to test the market. If it did well, she planned to put the item in stores across the country.

The buyer asked Karen for two hundred scarves. Without thinking, Karen said, "Sure. I'll have them in sixty days." But she had no manufacturer. She made all her scarves by hand.

Two friends from her knitting class helped her to produce the first order, but she knew she could not keep up with the demand. Karen worked night and day to deliver her product. At the same time, she feverishly cruised the Internet looking for suppliers and manufacturers. She quickly realized that her price point was too low to use an American manufacturer, so she started looking abroad.

After signing with an overseas manufacturer, she thought she'd solved the problem. But because of her inexperience, she didn't factor in the time it takes overseas items to clear customs. Due to the delay, she missed her shipment to the department store. The store canceled her order. In the end, she lost a great deal of money on the transaction.

Author Stephen R. Covey said, "Begin with the end in mind." When you design your business, you must decide how much you can take on, and how big you want your operation to become, and plan accordingly.

Why Does It Take Twelve Months to Plan?

What's special about a twelve-month timeline for starting a small business? After coaching thousands of entrepreneurs and talking with small business experts across the country, and as I considered all of the expensive mistakes I had made early on in my first business, I developed the Emerson Planning System, a twelve-month process to transition from corporate America to small business ownership.

To see why it takes a year, ask yourself if you have:

- A 750 or higher credit score
- Zero debt (including no car payments; mortgage and student loans are exceptions)

Then consider if you have the following cash reserves:

- Twelve months' salary in emergency savings
- Twelve to twenty-four months of monthly budget to run your household
- The first year of operating expenses to start the business

Catch your breath. These are the financial requirements for starting a business! Repositioning yourself financially may take a year or more. There's no shortcut. When you first start out in business, your personal credit is your business's credit.

Credit

Banks typically do not extend loans or lines of credit until you've been in business two to three years. There are a few franchises you can buy into that provide lending support, but it is still rare for a start-up to be able to borrow money beyond a microloan from an alternative lender. In the beginning, your credit cards, home equity, 401(k), savings, and loans from family and friends are all you will have to start, then hopefully your next funding will come from your customers. You might also consider pursuing crowdfunding, but that's a hard way to raise money to start a small business.

And this doesn't take into account the time needed to develop your life plan, validate your business idea, develop your marketing strategy and your business plan, and get in place all the elements of your day-to-day operations. As you move through this book, you'll see why it's a twelve-month timeline.

Consider these statistics:

- It takes typically eighteen to twenty-four months for a small business to break even and three years to earn a profit.
- Less than 10 percent of all small businesses in the United States gross over $1 million in revenue.
- 20 percent of small business owners will go out of business within the first year of operation.
- 50 percent will go out of business by their fifth year in business.

For these reasons, think carefully about timing your decision to quit your job. You're doing yourself no favors by leaving your job prematurely. Start as a side hustle first. The twelve-month planning system is a plan for long-term success.

Additional Resources

Over the years, I have become so concerned about building up the business skills of would-be entrepreneurs that I have written over five thousand articles and developed three online courses about how to start and stay in business. Head to my website to check out all the resources: https://succeedasyourownboss.com.

EMERSON'S essentials

You need to develop a life plan before you ever write a business plan. You need to make sure you are clear about what you want for your life and why. Too many entrepreneurs underestimate and romanticize what is required to run a small business. Starting your own business will cause a radical shift in your lifestyle; you need to think through what this will mean. If you start a catering business that specializes in weddings, that means you'll work a lot of weekends. If you have kids that have a lot of weekend activities, that could cause conflict. You want to start a business that is good for you and your family. Only after you've clarified family goals and needs are you ready to get into the nitty-gritty of your business planning.

What If You Don't Have Twelve Months?

A year to plan and launch your business is ideal. Have people done it more quickly? Sure. Sometimes people are forced to start sooner. They're laid off, get fired, or receive great early retirement packages. Needing an immediate source of revenue, they put their enterprises on the fast track.

If you live by a budget, have your debt under control, and have accumulated a significant amount of savings, you may well be able to start your business in less than twelve months. Others may take more than a year to get their personal finances in order. But the point is that with such a tight economy, no entrepreneur can afford to waste time or resources, or to make too many expensive mistakes. Once you start, you will get some on-the-job training, but that's a luxury, and you can't afford to waste it on things you should have known before you opened your doors. The Emerson Planning System gives you time to evaluate your life, gain control over your finances, validate your business concept, determine your target customer, and then start a business while you are still working.

Hard Times Bring Great Innovations

Do not get discouraged in tight economic times. Great inventions and businesses have developed during difficult times in US history. Major companies today, including General Motors, Ocean Spray, Burger King, Microsoft, FedEx, Trader Joe's, Uber, and Airbnb, were all started during the Great Depression or the subsequent recessions (which happen roughly every ten years).

Think of this book as a reference guide. It walks you through each phase—from your first brilliant idea, through life planning, developing your financial plan or repositioning, evaluating your business concept, developing a marketing plan, writing your business plan, and launching your busines, and up through your first year of operations. Getting started down the path of entrepreneurship starts with a timely idea, then putting a proper business structure around it. Your time and money are on the line, and so are your dreams. Don't put them at risk by not doing enough market research and thoughtful planning.

This is a great time to explore your entrepreneurial side; you just need to make sure that the business you start is a solid business opportunity. This planning process may seem like an exercise, but it's really an opportunity to think everything through. This book will help you personally plan, grow, and research your business idea to make sure you are ready to meet the challenge of starting and running your small business.

PART I
Get Ready!

CHAPTER 3

GET YOUR LIFE PLAN
TOGETHER

Twelve Months Before You Start

What is a life plan? It's a way to identify your motivation, skills, and personal goals. Essentially, it's how you figure out what you really want out of life. When you start a business, it must align with your personal and professional goals. Developing a life plan is the best way to achieve that. Before your business opens its doors, there are eleven questions you must answer. You probably won't have answers for all of them right away, but over the next twelve months keep coming back to this list until you do.

- Why do I want to start a business?
- Do I have the entrepreneurial mindset?
- Do I have the energy and discipline to start this business?
- How much money do I need to make to be happy?

- Do I have a supportive spouse or family?
- How long can my household operate without my generating an income?
- What do I know about the industry and what do I need to learn?
- Is there a demand for my product or service?
- How is my product different from the competition?
- Do I have the confidence and skill to run a business?
- Do you know what kind of business you should start?

Just the Facts

When you start to consider your life plan and what you want your new life to look like, you can't succumb to emotion. You need to stay focused on the facts and separate them from your feelings. Here's a story to illustrate this point:

Among my early coaching clients were the owners of a restaurant and catering company. The husband was the chef, while his wife kept an eye on operations. Neither had a business background. Their food was great, and they had a good reputation, but their enterprise consistently operated in crisis mode.

I suggested they find a partner or investor, preferably someone with experience in the food industry. The wife was all for it, but the chef was a proud man. He agonized over relinquishing financial control to an investor. He delayed making a decision until he was nearly in financial ruin. Eventually he brought in an investor to save his business.

The chef couldn't separate his desire for control from the need for someone in the business with stronger entrepreneurial skills. As a result, he ruined his personal credit and almost wrecked his business.

EMERSON'S essentials

Business decisions must be made on the basis of factual financial data and not emotion. Successful entrepreneurs keep up-to-date financial records and let the facts and their budget drive business decisions.

I knew a woman who quit her corporate job to start a franchise. She was very excited and couldn't wait to pick out her location, develop her marketing plan, and open her doors. She told everyone about her new business. Two years went by, and I bumped into the woman and asked how it was going. She said, "I sold my business. I realized that I cannot be a slave to anything, especially something that doesn't fulfill me. On top of that, I hated managing teenagers. It was a bad deal all the way around. I'm now grateful to be back in a corporate job."

If this woman had taken the time to think through a life plan before starting the business, she probably never would have bought the franchise. You must fully understand your motivations up front, so that you can figure out how best to set up your business and the level of commitment it will take. Your business plan must align with your life plan. If it doesn't, the business will fail you.

EMERSON'S essentials

Everyone has tangible skills, but not everyone has all the skills needed to run a business. Thinking through your life plan will help you determine the lifestyle you want to live, but you also should learn your boss profile. I created a short survey to produce a nine-page report that will reveal your entrepreneur type, work style, leadership style, sales capabilities, ideal business model, and if you need a partner or should consider a franchise. If you want to clarify what business you should start, take my Boss quiz at https://smallbizlady.lpages.co/bossquiz/.

People who have an entrepreneurial mindset are typically motivated by five basic things:

1. Control
2. Freedom
3. Money
4. Problem solving
5. Creativity

The trick is to determine which one motivates you the most. Ask yourself which of the following best describes your personality and your attitude toward work. Based on this information, you will be able to set up your company in a way that works best for you.

- **Control: You want to do things your way.** You like power and influence. You are highly self-motivated. You want to have control over the products and/or the operations. The question you struggle with is…how much control? Do you need it on a day-to-day basis, or is it enough to control the strategic direction of the company? You struggle to balance micromanagement with delegation.
- **Freedom: Flexibility is what you desire.** You want to be in control of your life and how you work. You might be disillusioned with your job because you're not allowed to telecommute or work flextime hours. You need to determine where and when you work. Work/ life balance is a major focus for you. You are driven by deadlines and results, but not necessarily by structure.
- **Money: You have calculated how much money you make for your employer, and you believe you could and should be making the same amount for yourself.** All entrepreneurs want and need to make money. But how much is enough? Are you looking to create a lifestyle business to provide a decent income and a couple of nice vacations a year, or do you want to buy your own island? Your answer will determine what kind of capital you will need and when. Whatever the case, you're clear that money is your main motivating factor.
- **Problem solving: You are a solution-oriented thinker.** You want to help people. You like a challenge and are a risk-taker. This is good, since clients want solutions. On the downside, you have a tendency not to focus on finishing tasks. You have multiple projects going at one time. Over the long term, you sometimes struggle with a lack of focus.

■ **Creativity: You are a big-idea person.** You want your business and its products to be your legacy. You are all about innovation and process development. You believe there is a new and better way to do most things. At times, you neglect or resent feedback on your creative ideas, even if it might lead to improvement. At the same time, you're highly protective of your intellectual property so that someone else will not get the primary financial benefit from your great idea.

Rate yourself for each of these traits by giving it a number from 1 to 5, with 5 being Extremely Important and 1 being Not Important. This exercise will show your hierarchy of motivations.

ENTREPRENEURSHIP MOTIVATION SCALE

Trait	Rating
Control	_____
Freedom	_____
Money	_____
Problem solving	_____
Creativity	_____

Construct Your Life Plan

With this exercise, you've determined what motivates you. Now you need to see what that says about your plans to become an entrepreneur. I suggest you consider discussing this with your spouse or a group of close friends. Here are some further questions to get you started:

■ **What is your passion? Is there an industry that fits your passion?** Think about the types of things that you love to do, whether at work or at home. Do you have any hobbies that could be businesses? What would you do for free?

- **What do you know how to do?** This is not a standard resume list. Instead, think back over all the jobs you've held. List all of your job skills and accomplishments in exhaustive detail. Take note of accomplishments in your professional and personal life. Don't forget to include volunteer activities. Consider the skills you have that would be helpful in starting a business and managing it successfully.

- **In what way(s) are you a rock star?** Are you a "killer" salesperson? An excellent project manager? Are you an idea guy? A great customer relationship manager? A number cruncher? Or, better yet, a technical wiz who's also a "killer" salesperson?

- **What do you do really, really well that you could sell?** Now think about the other skills you have that could be a business. What have you been trained to do? Do you do taxes? Tutor college students? Make furniture? Bake amazing pies and cakes? Build home improvements? Are you big into blockchain and cryptocurrency? Do you enjoy working out?

- **What do you hate to do?** Sometimes what you are trained in is not something you particularly like to do. If something makes your brain feel dead, you shouldn't make a business of doing it even if you excel at this activity. In the long run, you'll burn yourself out and your business will fail.

- **Do you get bored easily?** If so, rule out businesses that involve doing the very same thing for every customer. You will need a business that has a different challenge every day.

- **What is your energy level?** How long can you work at a stretch? For start-ups, fourteen- to sixteen-hour days are not uncommon. Consider your age and how family obligations will impact your energy level. Are you a parent with young children or aging parents? Are you over fifty? Can you handle a start-up business and the administration of your household?

- **What are your technical skills?** In today's fast-paced world, technology changes faster than the blink of an eye. Consider things such as your knowledge of social media, content, photography, customer relationship management (CRM) software, email, marketing automation, inventory management systems, project management software, e-commerce websites, mobile web strategies, voice search, and accounting software. Can you see yourself entering your own data into QuickBooks? Are you a technophobe, or eager to learn new things? Social media marketing is a great way to launch a new business, but the technology is changing constantly. Do you currently use Instagram, LinkedIn, Twitter, Facebook, YouTube, Pinterest, TikTok, or Clubhouse? How are your graphics skills? How about your blogging skills? Can you manage a WordPress website? Can you edit podcasts, and record YouTube videos with a smartphone? If you can't operate the technology, the only alternative is hiring help or learning it. Can you afford technical help? Do you have the patience to learn?

EMERSON'S experience

Following is an excerpt from my list of skills:

- Supervised teams as large as twenty-five people, including graphic designers, writers, photographers, web developers, and animators.
- Developed various marketing projects for broadcast or business use.
- Developed and established company-wide policies and operating plans consistent with broad company objectives.
- Directed and guided the planning and management of the company's production, research, and development activities.

Now do another exercise. This one you can do by yourself. Take thirty minutes and write down what your best day will look like five years from now.

Be bold! Consider things like ultimate vacations, the house you want, hobbies, volunteer work, philanthropy, and early retirement goals. Leave out no detail. Specify everything down to what color the limousine is that picks you up and takes you to the airport to fly to your summer home in southern Spain. (Okay, that was a small window into my vision, but you get the point.) After you are done, create a vision board poster, using old magazines. You need to have a physical reminder of your goals for your life and your business.

Your Ideal Work Setting

You have already considered your personal goals and motivations, realities of your life, and the skills you have and need to run your business. It's time to figure out what kind of environment you like to work in.

- Do you need to be around people?
- Can you work from home, or do you need a structured office?
- Do you need flex hours to balance taking care of your family?
- How many days a week will you work in your business?

Following is a work style chart. In the boxes, rate each of the issues according to its importance by giving it a number from 1 to 5, with 5 being Extremely Important and 1 being Not Important. You'll be able to see from this what kind of setting you want to work in.

WORK STYLE SURVEY

- ❏ I want to work a four-day workweek _____
- ❏ I am willing to work a six-day workweek _____
- ❏ I want to work from home _____
- ❏ I want to work from an office _____
- ❏ I want to work in an office setting with other people _____
- ❏ I prefer to work behind the scenes _____
- ❏ I like interacting with lots of people _____
- ❏ I prefer limited travel _____
- ❏ I don't mind lots of travel _____

Now you have an idea of where you want to go, what skills you already have and need, and what type of work setting suits you best. This information will also let you see whether your business goals and your personal preferences are compatible. If you only want to work four days a week, running a retail store with long hours may not be for you.

Make a list of steps you need to take to achieve your life goals. Refer to this list often during the next twelve months. Your life plan will keep you focused so you can do what you love—and that always brings out the best in an entrepreneur.

Finding the Right Business Idea

Some entrepreneurs are born; they are the types who just can't work for other people. Some entrepreneurs are made through years of working soul-sapping jobs, and finally one day they just get brave enough to leave; they know they can make more money working for themselves. Some people grow up in a family business and it falls into their lap or they are strong-armed into taking over the business by their parents. Others are forced into business ownership after months of frustration looking for a job. Regardless of how you make your decision to join the ranks of the self-employed, the next question is: What business should you start?

There are many paths, but it really boils down to four options:

1. Start a service business from scratch
2. Buy an existing business
3. Buy a franchise
4. Create an e-commerce business

If you want to start a business organically, you will need to develop your business idea and be clear that you have a viable market. In other words, you need to know who is buying and why, to see if you can identify the right business for you.

The question of what kind of business to start is one of the toughest you'll face. In order to answer this question, consider the following.

First, look back at the results from the life planning exercises earlier in this chapter.

■ What are your passions?
■ Where are you a rock star?
■ What would you do for free?
■ Is there a business that fits your passion?

Analyze the hard and soft skills you have that would be helpful in launching and managing a business. A small business owner may have to take on many roles initially, so if your skills list has a scattershot of expertise, do not be discouraged; the variety will be to your advantage.

Take a few days to play with the list. In essence, you are creating an abstract that describes the skills and experience you bring to your new role as a small business owner. Your answers to these questions help you identify what fascinates you and what your current abilities are. If there is little overlap between the two—for example, you love jewelry design but have little knowledge of the practicalities of selling your jewelry—you may have work to do.

Then, go deeper...

- What are your strongest skills?
- Are you highly self-disciplined or do you need structure?
- What do you know that you can sell?
- What service can you provide?
- What do you want to avoid doing if at all possible?
- What keeps you interested?
- How much time can you devote to your new endeavor?
- Do you have any technical skills?

This level of analysis will help you identify your skills. It's a crucial step in the process because you need a business that can leverage your skills. For example: If you want to be a website designer and have artistic training and programming knowledge, but don't know your way around accounting software, you're going to have to either learn the software or outsource your invoicing.

If you have skills in an area that you find mind-numbingly boring, don't start a business doing that. Find more fulfilling work. Maybe a franchise would be better for you, because they train you to run the business. Depending on what you want to do, it may even require going back to school to get an additional degree or certificate to redefine your expertise.

Another question to ask yourself, and answer honestly: Do you have the ability to work six to eight or more hours a day for your start-up, with no pay?

This is the time to think critically in order to tease out answers that can provide meaningful direction to determine what type of business you should pursue. You need to get clear about the problem you want to solve, what you want, and then what you're willing to commit to so you can accomplish your goals.

Now, let's get moving…

- Are you energized or depleted by other people?
- Are you a hard worker or burned out from corporate life?
- Do you want to work only as little as necessary?
- Are you fit to work from home?
- Do you want to be the center of attention or work behind the scenes?
- Do you want structured hours or flexibility?

The answers to this set of questions will give you information to help you establish if your dreams and your reality are compatible. If you want to have a retail location, but also desire flexibility and to work from home, there is a major disconnect between your wants and the scope of the type of business you desire. Of course, there are workarounds to many of these challenges, but it may require more capital to realize a solution, which will inform you of how deep your pockets will need to be to get started successfully.

These exercises are critical in helping you to define the type of business that you can successfully develop. You can start a professional service business, buy an existing business, invest in a franchise, start a retail or online business; there are many business models to choose from.

Give yourself a deadline for working through these questions and push through even if it feels like you are not revealing compelling information. Remember, entrepreneurs must be very self-motivated, so if you're having difficulty completing this task on your own, that may reveal that you might not be ready for what it takes to launch your dream business. Stay on track to discover a great business idea.

EMERSON'S action steps

1. Spend quality time with yourself and develop your life plan. Discover how you really want to live!
2. Find visual images of your life plan and make a vision board collage.
3. Keep your vision board in a visible place to constantly remind you of why you are working so hard. Tape it on the wall in your workspace or make it a screen saver.
4. When making strategic decisions about your new business venture, begin by reviewing your life plan to ensure that your business goals remain in alignment with your personal goals.
5. Learn your business profile at https://smallbizlady.lpages.co/bossquiz/.

CHAPTER 4

Construct a Financial Plan

As you prepare to leap into entrepreneurship, you must focus on your finances. This will require some long discussions with your partner and children as you decide how to scale down your lifestyle. This means having a clear, thought-out plan, one that your family will support. In this chapter, we'll consider just how to construct such a plan. Start with a realistic evaluation of your financial situation and then decide what the financial demands of your business will be.

Your Personal Financial Goals

Ideally, you should achieve four personal financial goals prior to starting your business:

1. Zero debt (except your mortgage and student loans)
2. Credit score should be 750 or higher
3. Twelve to twenty-four months of household expenses in savings
4. First year of working capital for the business

Eliminate Personal Debt

Eliminating your debt will allow you to make decisions that are always in the best interest of your business and not due to pressure from creditors. Zero debt will enable you to free up your credit capacity. You will probably not be able to eliminate your mortgage or student loans, but everything else needs to go, especially credit cards. Pay off your car. Get down to basic living expenses only, i.e., mortgage, phone, gas, electric, cable, food, etc. Consider a home equity loan (if you decide to do this, you must apply while you are still working and can prove income) so you can pay off every bill you have, including your car loan.

EMERSON'S experience

One of my classmates from Virginia Tech is a Shell Oil franchisee. When he first wanted to join the oil giant, he was told that the cost was $900,000 to lease one gas station. He figured he was a smart guy with a good business plan driven by a franchising opportunity with a *Fortune* 100 company. He had an excellent business background and exceptional personal credit. He went to a few banks to borrow the money, and every single one turned him down. This often happens to start-up entrepreneurs. Banks typically are only interested in loaning money to businesses with a two- to three-year track record.

After being rejected by the third bank, he decided to come up with the money on his own. Fortunately, since his first job out of college he had saved

25-40 percent of every paycheck he ever made. He owned two houses, so he sold them both. He was an investor in an Internet business, and he sold his interest in that. He sold his car. He opened several new credit cards and took the cash advances on them. He was still short of the money he needed, so he went to his father for help. His parents took out a second mortgage on their house. As a family, he and his parents came up with the $900,000 to acquire the first gas station. Within five years, they had twenty gas stations. They have now diversified into food franchises and are owners of a $180 million family business. The moral of this story is people who have assets have options.

Credit Card Management

When it comes to eliminating credit card debt, finance expert Vanessa A. Lindley says there are three methods to get out of debt:

1. **The Snowball Method:** Arrange the debts by balance, from smallest to largest, and beat down the smallest one first.
2. **The Avalanche Method:** Order the debt from the highest to the lowest interest rates, and beat down the one with the highest interest rate first.
3. **The Snowflake Method:** Add unexpected "extra" money like bonuses or tax refunds to help pay off debt using either of the previous methods.

You must do this while at the same time continuing to pay the minimum fees on the other cards to keep them current. And keep your credit cards once you've paid them off. Don't cut up your cards or cancel them. You will need those credit lines for your business. It doesn't matter how many credit cards you have, as long as you don't use more than 30 percent of the available credit. You want to eliminate debt, increase your borrowing power, and protect your credit score at the same time.

Eliminate Monthly Payments

First, pay off obligations that will eliminate a monthly payment. For example, if you get a bonus of $5,000, use some of it to pay off the balance on your car. By doing so, you eliminate the $350 monthly payment from your household budget and increase your rate of savings.

Improve Your Credit Score

Exceptional credit is essential when starting out in business. You will be asking vendors and others to extend you credit. Before they do so, they will review your credit score—not your business, because that doesn't exist yet—your personal credit score. Your personal credit is your business's credit.

Before you sign a lease for retail space, the landlord will pull your credit score. If you ever plan to borrow money or apply for a line of credit, your personal credit score is the most important information in the application process.

Your score on the most commonly used index—the Fair Isaac Corporation, or FICO—ranges from 300 to 850. For your business to avoid credit problems in its early stages, your personal score should be at least 620; the ideal is 750 or higher. (FICO also has bankcard and auto credit categories; these scores can range from 250 to 900.)

Managing Your Household Budget

You must run your household using a monthly budget; it's the best way to keep track of your expenses. Many people shy away from budgets because they think that they are about limiting spending. Think again! A budget is about planning your spending. Creating your household budget should be a shared activity.

For it to work, you and your spouse or partner should create your budget together, understand its purpose, and agree upon its principles. Managing your household with a budget is a great skill to have because you will need to manage your business with a budget too.

EMERSON'S essentials

Take the time to get your budget right. Use www.mint.com to manage your budget and expenses online.

- Use budget software to help track your spending (make sure to record all receipts).
- Anticipate future expenses as much as possible.
- Have an accountability partner. Your spouse, a close friend, or a peer who can question you about a sudden shopping spree is who you want in this role.

To make a budget, take the following steps:

1. Write down your net income after taxes and deductions.
2. List all of your major expense categories (mortgage, car payment, etc.).
3. Total all expenses.
4. Subtract total expenses from income.
5. If a deficit appears, determine how to address it.

You can earn additional income to cover a deficit; possibly you or your spouse will need to get a second job for a while. You can make up the deficit out of your savings, but since your savings are limited, this is a losing game. Or you can reduce your expenses. If you're getting ready to start a business, the last option is probably the best.

SAMPLE BUDGET FOR A FAMILY OF FOUR
Monthly Expenses

Savings	$250
Mortgage	$2,500
Home equity loan	$200
Personal grooming	$150
Church donations	$100
Entertainment	$200
Dry cleaning	$60
Car note(s)	$480
Car maintenance and insurance	$225
Gas for two cars	$200
Food/household supplies	$600
Life insurance	$168
Prescriptions/co-pays	$120
Daycare/aftercare	$760
Electric/gas	$280
Phone/cable/Internet	$150
Cell phone(s)	$300
Water	$65
Children's activities costs	$255
Credit cards	$400
Total household costs	**$7,463**

Now you know what your monthly costs are. You also know that you must have twelve months of living expenses—or, in the previous case, $89,556—in reserve before you open your business.

EMERSON'S essentials

If you can run your household with a monthly budget, you are far more likely to run your small business with a budget. This will help you always stay on top of your company's expenses and profitability.

Personal Cash Reserves

In fact, to be completely financially secure in your new venture, remember the three pools of money you should have in a savings or money market account prior to starting your business:

■ Twelve months' salary in emergency savings
■ Twelve to twenty-four months of monthly budget to run your household
■ The first year of operating expenses for your business

Make sure you understand all of your current and future household expenses as well as those your business will incur. It will help to track your family expenses for a month. Once you do that, you can start looking at ways to cut back. If you start modifying your spending habits a year before you quit your job, it won't seem so drastic when your paycheck is gone.

Determine how you will cover additional insurance costs. Since most people's health insurance is through their work, quitting your job will mean you're responsible for your own insurance. There are several types of policies you may need once you quit your job: health, disability, business liability, workers' compensation, and life insurance.

Options for Health Insurance

It's possible you may not need to buy health insurance entirely on your own. There are these options:

- Use your spouse's insurance through his/her job.
- Consider COBRA, a federal law that requires employers with group health plans to offer former employees the opportunity to continue their health insurance for at least eighteen months. (This is an expensive option.)
- Pursue an individual or family policy. You may be able to buy health insurance as part of a group; trade associations and chambers of commerce are good sources for group policy options. Or try the Affordable Care Act's insurance marketplace at www.healthcare.gov; costs for available options there are based on income.
- Secure a business health insurance policy for yourself and your employees when you can afford it. Use an insurance broker to help research your options.

Disability insurance is an important consideration, especially for single-income families. If you do physical work in dangerous environments or if your business will involve heavy lifting (e.g., you plan to work as a contractor, painter, security agent, florist, etc.), disability insurance is a must.

EMERSON'S experience

When I was pregnant with my son, I had an extremely tough pregnancy. I was unable to work for nearly six months. I never could have imagined needing disability insurance, but I did. When you are an entrepreneur, if you do not work, you do not get paid.

Restructure Your Finances

As you move ahead with this part of your financial plan, take the following steps:

1. **Get your credit report.** TransUnion, Equifax, and Experian will each provide a free credit report once a year, but you must pay for your actual credit score. Get all three scores, as each credit bureau scores differently. You can also use www.creditkarma.com to get a free credit report.

2. **Calculate your net worth.** Net worth is your assets minus your liabilities. Make sure to include cash values of your cars and any whole life insurance policies as assets.

3. **Pay your bills on time.** Even if you don't have the full amount, send something, and send it on time. Paying late fees is like throwing money away. Shift your bill paying online. Many banks offer free online banking. You can also arrange for many of your regular monthly bills to be automatically deducted from your account.

Control Your Spending!

Some people make spending decisions based on what is in their pocket that day. Others treat their check card like free money. By living by a budget, you become the CEO of your money. You can take control of your spending. Use these simple rules to cut down excess spending and get a handle on other expenses.

- **Keep good records.** Keep separate records for your business and personal finances. Comingling funds is bad. Religiously track all income and expenses, and save all of your receipts. Many expenses are tax deductible.

- **Before heading to the store, make a list of what you need and stick to it.** Avoid impulse buying. Be careful not to go grocery shopping when you are hungry. A growling stomach makes it very hard to stick to your list.

- **Review and eliminate all unnecessary subscriptions.** Fees of $19.99–$65.00 a month might not seem like a lot of money, but are you even still using the app or service? Look at the cable and cell phone bills too. Are you watching all those streaming services you pay for?

- **Cut back on expensive snacking.** Freshly brewed coffee and movie popcorn are the best, but you can brew your own coffee and eat before you go to the movies. The money you spend each week on unnecessary extras can add up. Treat yourself once in a while, but don't make a daily habit of it. You'll be surprised how much money you'll save.

- **Avoid retail therapy.** It can get lonely on Saturday night, but stay away from online shopping to amuse yourself. You can no longer afford to buy something shiny and new to make yourself feel better. Instead, develop a low-cost or free hobby. Try yoga, start running, or take a long, hot bubble bath.

- **Review your insurance policies.** Consider increasing your deductibles on your car and homeowners and health insurance. This will reduce your monthly or quarterly premiums.

- **Cook at home and bring your leftovers to work for lunch.** Stop going out for lunch at work. You'll save money, eat healthier, and spend more quality time with your family.

- **Park and ride.** Weekly gas and parking expenses can add up. Consider using public transportation if it's available in your area. Talk to coworkers who live near you about carpooling.

- **Check out the library.** You can borrow books and magazines from the library and request special orders. If you're a serious book junkie, find a good used bookstore or buy used books online.
- **Try a staycation.** Rediscover your hometown. Hit the local news websites for what's going on around your town. Many cities sponsor free, low-cost, and family-friendly events.
- **Entertain at home.** Stop drinking alcohol in bars and restaurants. Beer, wine, and mixed drinks are cheaper when you pour them yourself. Pick up a six-pack or a few bottles, invite over some friends you haven't seen in a while, and hang out at the house.

Someone suggested, "You must ask yourself 'Why?' three times before you make any purchase." In other words, you should have three separate reasons that justify spending any of your precious (and limited) resources.

Start-Up Funds Strategies

Launching your business is going to cost money, and it probably can't all come from savings. You need to evaluate where you will raise your start-up funds.

Do You Have Any Investments You Can Liquidate?

If you have a stock account, cryptocurrency investments, a Roth IRA, or any real estate that you can sell, cash out, or borrow against, that could be a great source of start-up funds.

Determine How Much Equity You Have in Your Home

Equity is the market value of your home, minus any mortgages or credit lines in use. You can often tap in to that equity by getting a line of credit; the home equity loan serves as a second mortgage.

Determine How Much Money Your Employer Owes You

Do you have unused vacation/sick time, a bonus, or a buyout package? That's money you can cash out when you leave your current job.

Use the One-Third Rule

Whenever you get a bonus check, tax refund, or any occasional sudden money, spend one-third on something you need or want, put one-third toward paying down debt, and put one-third toward your saving plan.

Consider Crowdfunding

There are more than two thousand websites that allow you to build an online pitch so you can start pestering your friends and strangers for donations to fund your business. Keep in mind, the average crowdfunding campaign generates only $10,000.

Your saving plan starts with your ability to control spending and cut costs. You cannot kick an addiction to living from paycheck to paycheck all at once. It will be a gradual step-by-step process, but you can do it!

Before you implement these sweeping changes, have a family meeting to get buy-in from your partner or spouse and your children. Most importantly, be the change you want to see. Set an example and show that you are committed to your plan.

Your Banking Relationship

When your personal finances are in order, you need to begin setting up your banking arrangements for the business. Do not use the same bank for your personal and business affairs. If you use your personal bank as your business bank, you could lose everything if your business goes under, since the bank can seize your personal assets to satisfy your business debt.

EMERSON'S essentials

You are not just looking for a bank; you are looking for a banking relationship. You want to find a bank that is interested in your business success and not just your deposits. Select a bank that is best for your business.

Do not be swayed by TV advertising when selecting a lending institution. Remember that there's a big difference between the kind of services you'll need from your business bank and those you need from your personal bank.

Shop around. Seek referrals from your network. Interview at least three branch managers at different banks before making your decision. Larger banks have a tendency to rotate small business bankers frequently, so it's important to know what is happening at the branch that you will be using. Ask the following questions:

- How fast are checks cleared to my business account?
- Is there a dedicated small business banker on your staff?
- Are loan decisions made locally?
- How many Small Business Administration loans did your bank process last year?

Once you decide on a bank, meet with your branch manager once or twice a year to discuss the status of the business and any exciting news (e.g., business awards, major new clients/contracts, etc.). Bankers love this, and it keeps them engaged in your success.

EMERSON'S action steps

1. Build your credit score to 750 or higher.

2. Develop a plan to eliminate your debt.

3. Construct a household budget and stick to it.

4. Go cash only. It is psychologically harder to spend cash than credit. Do not use your credit cards, but debit cards are just fine. If you do not have the cash for a purchase, you don't need it.

5. Consult a financial planner or an accountant who works with small businesses to help you examine your overall financial requirements before starting your business.

6. Select the right bank for your business and set up an account. Do *not* use the same bank for your personal account and your business account.

CHAPTER 5

THINK LIKE A
BUSINESS OWNER

Eleven Months Before You Start

Someone said, "You are one idea away from accomplishing anything you want." This is true. Entrepreneurs are visionaries. They see the big picture. They are leaders and innovators.

Sometimes, though, their visions are too broad and grandiose. Instead of a million-dollar business, they want to become a billion-dollar company like Amazon. Confidence in your ability and your product or service is essential, but the business vision must be realistic. You need to define that vision by your solution and your core services or products, your unique value proposition, the year-to-year revenue and profit growth, and ultimately, how big you want the company to become long term.

Visualizing Your Business

Let's start by defining a small business. The Small Business Administration (SBA) has established two widely used criteria:

1. For most manufacturing and mining industries, the company can have a maximum of five hundred employees.
2. For most nonmanufacturing industries, average annual receipts should not exceed $7.5 million.

Go to www.sba.gov for more information about these standards.

Remember that you're starting a small business. Don't let your vision run away with you. There will be plenty of opportunity for growth. While self-confidence is essential, you must be careful not to give the appearance of overconfidence.

If you're successful, you will attract mentors by being approachable and responsive. Some mentors will be clients; others will be angel investors or retired executives who may see something in you they want to nurture.

EMERSON'S essentials

Stay humble. There are plenty of people who have forgotten more than you know about business. Use your attitude and excitement about your new enterprise to attract people to work for you, support you, and do business with you.

Here are seven essential principles of small business success:

- Have an entrepreneurial mindset.
- Observe strict fiscal discipline.

- Form a kitchen cabinet of advisors to support you.
- Have a defined brand identity and professional marketing collateral.
- Focus on a niche target market.
- Provide excellent customer service.
- Carefully manage your banking relationship.

The Entrepreneurial Mindset

Why does one small business owner flourish while another one fails? Because successful entrepreneurs develop the right mindset about their business. How you perceive your business and your life defines your reality. If you think you can or think you can't, both are true.

- Business owners with an entrepreneurial mindset seek to stand out in the crowd.
- Successful small business owners keep a positive attitude.
- Entrepreneurs are willing to fail in order to eventually win.
- Wise entrepreneurs learn from failure and move on quickly.

Each day we make hundreds of choices—they cause the results we experience. Your answers to the questions you ask yourself will determine the outcome of the day. To be a successful entrepreneur, you must not only get the right answers; you also need to make sure you're asking the right questions.

You must not be afraid to make a mistake. Sometimes you'll be doing your best but feel frustrated by a lack of progress. Every entrepreneur goes through these difficult periods. Times like these are when you need to focus on the positive and maintain your optimism. Those are also the times to reach out to your support network.

EMERSON'S essentials

My Dad always said, "We would not know good days if it were not for bad days." When challenges come, figure out the lesson that you were supposed to learn, and move on. You never lose in business—either you win or you learn. The key is to avoid negative thinking.

To change the outcome of each day, you must change the questions you ask yourself. Rephrase your questions in a positive fashion. Rather than, "What can I do to avoid being late?" ask, "How can I make sure I am on time?" Make sure your questions are not keeping you from reaching your goals. More than 50 percent of business problems are not very well disguised personal problems. Beware of "the cult of personality" business. Any company that kowtows to the owner's ego will ultimately fail.

You must hire smart people and empower them to make decisions, even if they are not always the decisions you would make. Remember, it's not always about you. It is about your family, your employees, and your customers.

Be a family-first entrepreneur. This means that you always have options, not obligations, and your family is always your number-one client. Don't let your business consume your life. Try to compensate your family for the fact that in the early years, you'll have to work very long hours.

Key to thinking like an entrepreneur is remaining focused. Here are some tips to motivate yourself:

- Develop a daily routine. Get up at the same time every day, exercise, and take a shower before you start work.
- Convert one room in the house into an office. Be aware that using a room with a bed makes naps inviting.

- Schedule breakfast meetings and early morning conference calls to get yourself going early.
- When you feel your energy getting low, take a dance break or take a walk around the block or get on a treadmill for thirty minutes.
- Avoid procrastination, perform follow-up activities right away. Send thank-you cards and email follow-ups quickly.
- Find an accountability partner that will call, text, or email to remind you about things you said you really needed to get done.

EMERSON'S essentials

Schedule when you will check email during your workday. If you open email first thing each day or start replying right away to your LinkedIn or other social media requests, you are working on someone else's agenda and not your own. Don't spend your work time on social media unless you are building your brand online.

Isolation is the enemy of entrepreneurship. Get some fellow business owner friends with whom you can talk regularly. You also may need to change your work environment from time to time. Always remain disciplined and stick to a schedule.

- Find a secondary workplace outside your home, e.g., a coffee shop, a bookstore, or the public library.
- Schedule your time. Plan when you will make sales calls, write checks, return calls, write blog posts, read email, and open mail.
- Make an action list at the end of every day to drive work activities for the next day.

- Do not make or accept personal calls during work hours, unless they're urgent. Explain to your friends and family about your work hours and make people respect them.
- Protect your work hours. Set aside one day a week to handle doctor's appointments and personal errands. Otherwise, do not run errands until after 6 p.m.
- Invest in a wireless headset so that you can multitask when answering your phone.

Get a Kitchen Cabinet of Advisors

Your kitchen cabinet is an unofficial board of directors for your business. They will brainstorm your business ideas and challenges. Include a variety of people who are invested in your success, such as an existing entrepreneur, a client or potential client, a lawyer, an accountant, and a mentor (with a significant network and a generous spirit). These people are already entrepreneurs or other businesspeople in a position to give you insight into what you need to do. Clients can provide valuable insights into budget cycles, current pain points, and other issues. Lawyers and accountants are always good business advisors. Mentors are there to provide leadership and sometimes emotional support, and they can introduce you to potential customers.

Pace Yourself

Sometimes when you look back over your day you'll find yourself focusing on what you didn't get done. That's not helpful. There is rarely enough time in a day to get everything done. The best thing to do is to prioritize and pace yourself. Even a marathon runner has to rest and refresh to keep going.

The early days in business are the toughest. Medical experts say we need to get seven to eight hours of sleep a night, and that's probably right.

But in the early days, while you are working your job *and* launching your business, a full night's sleep will be a luxury. Owning a business is great, but in the beginning it might own you. You have to fight the tendency of the business to take over your life.

Wherever you are, be present there. Do not be the parent at the ball field on your smartphone. The ups and downs of balancing life and work will sometimes have you turning yourself into a pretzel. But when you get that first sale, when you make enough profit to pay yourself a regular paycheck, sharing that moment with your family will be priceless. I get the biggest kick out of the fact that my son loves to tell people I'm the "Small-BizLady." Share your business with your family; it will be truly rewarding.

Be a Lifelong Learner

Successful business owners constantly seek to learn and evolve themselves. They hire coaches, take seminars, enroll in executive education and leadership programs, and approach life with the mindset that they need to learn something new every day. Don't ever stop. I even went back to school and got my MBA, since starting my business. As you become a successful business owner, you'll need to grow yourself.

Goals and Follow-Up

Successful business owners are good talkers, but they're even better with follow-up. They strive for completion, not perfection. They embrace change by breaking out of their comfort zone, challenging themselves and others.

Visionary leaders inspire those around them because they've thought long and hard about where they want their business to go and how to get there. If you want to be like them, set Specific, Measurable, Attainable, Realistic, and Timely goals (SMART goals).

Once you've worked to make all these things part of your daily routine, you'll be thinking like a successful business owner.

EMERSON'S action steps

1. List the seven essential principles of small business success and post the list somewhere you can refer to it often.
2. Be a family-first entrepreneur.
3. Avoid negative thinking. Keep a positive attitude.
4. Develop ways to motivate yourself and stay focused.
5. Develop a list of SMART goals.
6. Be a lifelong learner.

CHAPTER 6

CREATE YOUR BUSINESS MODEL

The next step in your timeline to becoming an entrepreneur is to refine your business concept. You must determine if your business idea is viable—that is, will it work as a business that will make money and eventually a profit? Ask yourself:

- Is there a need in the marketplace for my business?
- Who's the competition?
- What is my value proposition?
- How hard will it be to get my product to market?
- Is my product or service difficult to explain?
- Is my price point competitive?
- How will I meet the market demand?

- Does my business serve an unmet need?
- Does my product or service have staying power?
- Does my business idea have long-term growth opportunities?

Is There a Need in the Marketplace for Your Business?

Creating a business without validating the market is like driving to a new city without directions or Google Maps on your smartphone. You must make sure there's a real market you can sell to. Of course, you can also create a market need. In determining how to do this, quality market research is essential. Formal primary research (i.e., talking directly to consumers) is expensive; it's more affordable to do this thorough secondary research using the Internet, library, or industry reports.

Free Market Research Sites
- SBA's Office of Entrepreneurship Education
- US Census Data Tools and Apps
- Statista
- Pew Research Center
- Google Trends
- International Trade Administration

There are also fee-based market research sites; one of my favorites is D&B Hoovers.

Who's the Competition?
Your product or service will always have competition. The need you've identified in the market is being met somehow. If a new business owner tells you he has no competition, politely end the conversation and walk away. Perceived lack of competition means one of three things:

1. There is no real market for your product.
2. A monopoly controls the market so overwhelmingly that you can't even think of them as competition.
3. Your product does not exist. It's possible that you'll create a truly new product and industry (e.g., Apple changed the entire music industry with iTunes), but the chances of hitting the market in a major way with an innovation like this are slim for a self-funded small business without significant outside investment.

In the event of heavy competition, beware of market saturation. There may be no room for a new player. Say that in your neighborhood, drugstores are being built every few blocks—in some cases right across the street from each other. Should you become an independent drugstore owner in your town? Probably not.

Determining your competition requires market research. Who are your target customers? Teenagers? Millennials? Seniors? Young mothers? Other small businesses? How many potential customers do you have? Is your target market growing or shrinking? Gauging demand is an inexact science, but do yourself a favor and do thorough market research.

What Is Your Unique Value Proposition?

Your value proposition or competitive advantage is your company's unique skills implemented in a specific way to deliver your product or service. It is what draws customers to buy your product/service instead of your competitor's. Your potential clients must find an exceptional benefit in your product or service, but you can't rest there. Can you disrupt your market or industry? Harvard Business School professor Clayton Christensen defined disruption as "a process whereby a smaller company with fewer resources is able to successfully challenge established incumbent businesses." Erica Olsen, author of *Strategic Planning for Dummies*, claims that roughly 70 percent of all new products can be duplicated within one year, and 60–90 percent of process improvements will eventually be duplicated by competitors. Your competitive advantage needs to be sustainable. You can ensure that it is by continually developing and working on it. Dr. Christensen's disruptive innovation theory predicts that "when an entrant tackles incumbent competitors head-on, offering better products or services, the incumbents will accelerate their innovations to defend their business or soon be out of business." As the start-up, you must constantly innovate, and when you become the incumbent one day you must innovate to defend your market position. Strategy is about creating a unique value proposition that is not easily duplicatable by your competition.

How Hard Will It Be to Get Your Product to Market?

Do you have the money, manpower, manufacturing, and marketing to get your product to market? What technical expertise do you need to produce the product, and what distribution channels will you use to deliver it to the customer? Good businesses die every day due to lack of capital, insufficient distribution channels, or challenges with production or delivery. Make sure you consider what it will really take to make your business dream a reality.

Is Your Product or Service Difficult to Explain?

No one should be confused about why they should buy a product or service. If you are selling a disruptive product that could change your industry, you may need to spend the first year or two in business educating people. For example, it took some time for Apple to show its consumers how to use new features on the Mac computer. But the company's marketing campaigns were amazing. They made it cool to have one, so people started figuring out how to use them and then became unpaid evangelists for the Apple brand. A marketing campaign to make the market aware of an innovative product is not impossible, but it can be very costly.

Is Your Price Point Competitive?

When considering a price point for your product, survey the competition, but also know your own costs. Your price must cover all of your expenses, highlight the value you are providing the customer, and earn you a reasonable profit; it must also be competitive. Test your pricing strategy before going with it. The marketplace will quickly tell you if it's too high.

The wrong price will make a bad first impression. Often, you do not get a chance to make a second impression, so it's important to get this right. It's not always wise to be the cheapest offering. A salesperson once said their philosophy was to be the most expensive option in the market. It's a bold move, but if you spin it right, your customers will see real value in your offering.

Ultimately, pricing must be driven by your economics. If you don't make a profit, what is the point of having a business in the first place?

How Will You Meet the Market Demand?

If you have the hottest Christmas toy for children, your success hinges on cashing in on the opportunity before the season ends. What sort of lead time do you need to meet the demand? It may take several months to get new inventory, which may be too late. There will be many up-front cash obligations to respond to this kind of business demand, so cash flow management is critical.

Does Your Business Serve an Unmet Need?

Finding an unmet need in the marketplace can be a great business strategy. Many new ideas and products are built on existing concepts but fill an underserved niche, and you can quickly dominate a market. For example, the post office has always delivered packages, but FedEx and UPS took that concept to the next level.

A successful business solves a problem or fulfills a want or a need. Your marketing strategy should always focus on solutions. What problem does your customer need to solve?

Does Your Product or Service Have Staying Power?

You must know the difference between fads and trends. Fads are sudden changes in consumer behaviors that are here today, gone tomorrow. Think about Sony's PlayStation 5, Tickle Me Elmo, or the Cabbage Patch doll (a favorite from my childhood). All of these toys created holiday shopping nightmares for parents and bidding wars on eBay. Trends, on the other hand, are changes in the marketplace that will have a lasting impact. These types of businesses shift buyer behavior. Myspace started in 2003, which was the beginning of social networking. Facebook started in 2004, and Twitter started in 2006, which began a social media trend that has changed the world.

Capitalizing on a fad is tricky business. If you plan to start a fad business, you must make sure you can enter it quickly while the fad is hot, and that your product has enough staying power for you to make your money and cash out before the market moves again. It's better to track industry trends and figure out a product or service that takes advantage of a growing trend.

Are There Long-Term Growth Opportunities?

Does your business idea present the possibility of product line extensions in the future? If you're making homemade ice cream, will you create more flavors? If you make children's shoes, will you create a new line of children's rain boots or expand into women's footwear?

Do you have the resources to constantly improve your product line? Will you create an expanded model with more features? Is your product attractive to a global market? These are all questions that will determine how big your business can become.

Take Care of the Administrative Details

Once you've created a sound business concept—you know what you're going to make, how you're going to make it, and who you're going to make it for—you're ready to take the next step: You must create your business identity. That is, you must name the business and consult with a lawyer about the appropriate legal structure. Then you must incorporate your new venture. This process is important in protecting your business from legal and competitive issues.

Naming Your Business

Naming your business is tough. You want the name to be catchy and memorable, but you also want to be taken seriously. Most importantly, you want a name that will work now and in the future.

Using your last name, whether by itself or with words describing the business, is a good option. Further, if you use your last name in your business's name, you do not need to file the name with your state.

A fictitious name, also known as a trade name or assumed name, is any name, style, or designation other than the proper name(s) of the owner(s) of the business, and it should be registered as a fictitious name with your state government. If you decide to make up a name, it's best to find a name that encapsulates what you want people to think about your business. Examples of fictitious names include Shopify, Walmart, and Dunkin' Donuts.

Seven Tips for Naming Your Business

1. **Avoid a word that is hard to pronounce or spell.** It annoys people, and it will be harder for searchers to find your firm online.
2. **Do not create a new word.** It's never a good idea to have people scratching their heads wondering what a word means.
3. **Do not use a word so common that it is easily forget-table.** Always display your uniqueness to make your business memorable.

4. **If possible, avoid purposefully misspelled words.** Do not add numbers, odd letters, or dashes in your business name to make it work online.

5. **Do an online search to check your business name.** See if the URL is available. If someone is using your name, you have two choices: Find another name or create the URL with "inc," "online," or "llc" after it. You can also create a URL that describes what you sell, e.g., www.delawarelawncare.com.

6. **Do not use the name of your town.** PNC Bank was once Pittsburgh National Corporation. The name changed after the company expanded to multiple states. A name tied to your town can stifle your growth once you look outside your immediate region for customers.

7. **Once in business,** if you realize that your name no longer works—change it. A name change is a great PR hook and an excuse to hold a party to celebrate.

If you operate a business under a fictitious name, you must register in the state where you plan to do business. The purpose is to create a public record of who owns the business in order to protect the public from fraud. You also want to establish a date of name use in case you need to file for trademark protection. Depending on the state where you operate, there are penalties for failing to register a fictitious name. Registering your fictitious name does not provide your business with any exclusive rights to use the name. You must get it trademarked for that protection.

When you incorporate your business, you earn the exclusive use of your corporate name in your state. Your corporate name may not be the same as, or confusingly similar to, the name of any other business.

Creating Your Legal Structure

You want to protect yourself legally while accomplishing your business goals. Your structure should reflect the kind of business you want and the size of your enterprise.

When it is time to incorporate, you will need around $500 to incorporate a business. You can use an online company such as www.corpnet.com to establish your business entity. You will need to consult an accountant, since different legal entities have different tax implications.

Once you are incorporated, you will receive a corporate kit, which may include articles of incorporation, bylaws, your first meeting minutes, any stock certificates issued, and your corporate seal. Once you receive your official Employer Identification Number (EIN) letter from the IRS, store it in a safe place with these records.

The most common forms of legal entities are sole proprietorship, partnership, limited liability company (LLC), subchapter S corporation, and corporation. However, most small businesses opt for a single- or dual-member LLC entity.

Sole Proprietorship

A sole proprietorship is not a legal entity. There is no distinction between the owner and the company. You are personally responsible for the company's debts and, more importantly, you can be held personally liable for any lawsuits filed against the company. As owner, you can report the business's profit or loss on personal income tax returns.

Partnership

In a partnership, two or more people come together jointly to own and operate a business. They share the same personal liability as the sole proprietorship. All aspects of running the business are shared among the partners, and each partner is personally liable for the business debt.

Partnerships do not pay taxes but must file an informational tax return; each partner reports their financials from the business on their personal tax return. If you are going to have a partner, be sure to have a legal partnership agreement.

Limited Liability Company (LLC)

This is a partnership that limits the liabilities of the business to the amount of investment by each partner. No personal assets are at risk. The LLC is generally considered a good option for small businesses because it combines the limited personal liability feature of a corporation with the tax advantages of a sole proprietorship. Owners can report the business financials on their personal tax returns, or the LLC can elect to be taxed like a corporation. LLCs do not offer stock and are not required to observe corporate formalities, such as filing annual meeting minutes. Owners are called members, and the members manage the LLC.

Subchapter S Corporation (S-corp)

A subchapter S corporation provides limited liability and significant tax benefits for its owners. Profits are only reported on the business owner's personal tax return. The catch here is that the shareholder, if working for the company and if there is a profit, must pay him/herself wages and must meet standards of "reasonable compensation." In other words, you must pay yourself what you would have to pay someone else to do your job. If you do not do this, the IRS can reclassify all of the earnings and profit as wages, and you will be liable for all of the payroll taxes on the total amount. S-corps involve a significant paperwork burden and are limited to thirty-five stockholders.

Corporation

A corporation is a legal business entity that is separate from its owners. It can be private or publicly held. A corporation can be taxed, it can be sued, and it can enter into contractual agreements. The owners of a corporation are its shareholders. The shareholders elect a board of directors to oversee the major policies and decisions. The corporation has a life of its own and does not dissolve when ownership changes.

Which of these legal structures you choose depends on what you're selling, the size of your company, your investors' preferences, and other key factors.

EMERSON'S action steps

1. Answer these questions to determine whether your business idea is viable:
   - Who is your target market?
   - What business are you in?
   - Where will you sell your product/service?
   - When will you make a profit?
   - What is your competitive advantage?
   - How will you promote your business?
2. Think long and hard about your business name.
3. Turn your business into a legal entity for your protection.

CHAPTER 7

LINE UP A LAWYER AND AN ACCOUNTANT

You always need to make sure you are operating legally and that your business model is financially viable. A lawyer can advise you on your business incorporation, contracts, lease agreements, intellectual property protection, and other elements critical to your business. An accountant or bookkeeper will help you develop your initial financial projections and a budget, track monthly revenues and expenses, set up your accounting software, and keep you on top of your tax liabilities and quarterly tax payments.

How to Hire an Attorney

When it is time to incorporate your business, you need to engage an attorney. She will advise you on incorporation as well as whether you will need to secure patents, trademarks, or copyrights on your logo, slogan, systems, written materials, or products. Your attorney should review any contracts you are asked to sign, especially any leases, customer agreements, or loan documents. The lawyer should also draft the contract that you will use for your customers to engage services, any employment contracts, and your noncompete and nondisclosure agreements that all employees and strategic partners should sign.

It's best to hire a lawyer who has experience with small businesses, but you also want to make sure that your business consultant is responsive and has time for you. If you are considering purchasing a business or buying into a franchise, look for a lawyer who specializes in franchise agreements.

EMERSON'S essentials

You should feel comfortable with your lawyer and not intimidated. Look for experts who are smart, collaborative, and informative, and, most of all, will listen to you. Look for vendors who can help get more business.

If you select a lawyer from a large law firm, you may not get the one-on-one attention you need as a start-up business, and you are guaranteed to get a big bill.

Whoever you decide to use, check their qualifications. You can review the attorney's credentials on your state bar's website or use www.martindale.com. Make sure that the attorney is licensed and admitted to practice before the courts in your state. The state bar records will also inform you if the attorney has ever been reprimanded or involved in any illegal activity. Ask for referrals. Many small business development centers have partnerships with law schools and the local bar association to offer pro bono advice to start-up businesses. When selecting an attorney, interview at least three candidates. Ask them for small business references, and make sure that you check them.

Here are some questions for a potential lawyer:

- Do you need a large retainer to get started?
- What is your fee schedule for routine and nonroutine services?
- Will you provide itemized bills?
- What is your typical response time?
- What is the best way to reach you?
- Have you worked with any businesses in my industry?
- Can you provide three small business references?
- Can you give me an example of how you have helped clients secure business opportunities?
- Can I call you on any legal problem?

Get Ready for Business Taxes

In order to be in business, you must obtain an Employer Identification Number (EIN) from the Internal Revenue Service. The number is also known as a Federal Tax ID Number and identifies a business on a tax return. You also need an EIN number to open a business bank account unless you are a sole proprietor with no employees; in that case, you can use your Social Security number.

You need to get an EIN number if you:

- Incorporate your business
- Have a payroll service
- Have a SEP IRA or self-employed retirement plan
- File any employment; excise; fiduciary; or alcohol, tobacco, and firearms tax returns

You can secure the number easily at www.irs.gov.

How to Hire an Accountant

The next critical resource you will need is a good accountant. There are three levels of accounting experts you can hire: a bookkeeper, an accountant, and a certified public accountant (CPA). The main differences between these providers are their hourly rates and the level of services they provide small business owners.

A Bookkeeper

This person will set up your accounting software and enter receipts and invoices into your software weekly or monthly, handle payroll data and quarterly taxes, and create your monthly financial statements (income statements, balance sheets, cash flow statements). Bookkeepers are primarily accounting clerks responsible for recording accounting transactions and reconciling your bank statements. Bookkeepers typically do not prepare business tax returns. They also may not have the knowledge to help analyze your financial position. They may have two- or four-year business or accounting college degrees or just on-the-job training.

An Accountant

An accountant is qualified to handle the day-to-day bookkeeping needs of your company. He or she will set up your accounting software, accounts payable and accounts receivable charts, prepare payroll data and reporting requirements, and prepare other monthly financial statements. Accountants can also prepare business taxes. Accountants generally have college degrees and are trained to interpret and analyze financial data. They have a higher skill level and a higher hourly rate than bookkeepers.

A Certified Public Accountant (CPA)

This is an accountant who has passed a rigorous state examination. Only CPAs can certify an audit. CPAs provide all levels of accounting and consulting services and prepare tax returns. CPAs also provide tax planning and are highly qualified experts in accounting. As such, they are expensive.

You want an accountant who has experience with small businesses and your industry. You also need to make sure that your business consultant is patient and responsive because you may have a lot of questions starting out. Your accountant should be easy to talk to and good at explaining your accounting software as well as unfamiliar terms such as depreciation, chart of accounts, cost of goods sold, and balance sheets. For a small business, a smaller accounting firm or a solo practice is probably a better choice instead of a large accounting firm, because costs are generally lower and service is better. Shop around until you find the right fit. New tax laws are passed every year and some expire, so your tax professional who does your business taxes needs to be someone who would know about any changes. You tax preparer may not be the same person who does your monthly accounting and reconciliation.

Here's a list of questions that you should ask a candidate you are considering:

- What accounting software do you use?
- Do you provide software setup?
- Do you provide monthly bookkeeping, or do you have a preferred list of vendors we should use?
- What is your hourly rate?
- Will you prepare a contract with a set monthly fee?
- Can you provide three small business references?
- Do you work onsite at the client location?
- Do you work with many start-up businesses?
- What industries do you specialize in?
- Have you worked with any businesses in my industry?
- Do you also prepare business taxes?

One of the first things your accountant will need to do is help you create your operating budget and sales projections for your business plan (see Chapter 9).

Your accountant will recommend the kind of accounting software you should purchase. If you are comfortable with computers, there are a wide variety of computer programs on the market to help you manage your accounting, including QuickBooks, FreshBooks, Xero, and Sage. Many programs offer a free thirty-day trial. Ask your accountant which software makes the most sense for your business.

None of the programs will work, however, if you do not input your information on a regular basis. Use your accounting software to track all sales, invoices, receipts, and any payroll. You should also keep physical copies of all receipts, invoices, and canceled checks. It's a good habit to keep a notebook in your car to track your business mileage. Some people attach a little notepad to their dashboard.

Consult with your accountant to learn about the various state and local tax issues for your business. These include potential deductions and any requirements for paying estimated taxes and hiring employees. If you are going to have employees, or just for yourself, it may make more sense to engage a payroll service. It's always helpful as a self-employed person to have proof of your income.

EMERSON'S essentials

Payroll taxes are very complicated and confusing. Before you start a business, be sure to check the zoning restrictions in your area, particularly if you plan to be home based. There could be possible restrictions in your neighborhood on the kind of business you intend to run. Be sure to secure any business licenses required to operate your business.

Sales Taxes

Here are some basic rules for determining whether you are required to charge sales tax on your products or services.

Manufacturing Sales Are Tax-Exempt

If your company processes a product, then resells it in a different form, you are considered a manufacturer. Anything that is directly used in the manufacturing process is considered tax-exempt in most states. This doesn't mean that everything used in your business is tax-exempt; it only applies to the products that actually are used to develop your finished goods. For example, if you manufacture health and beauty products, all of the bottles, tubes, labels, ink, and shrink wrap used to produce the products are tax-exempt, but the packaging materials to ship the product are not.

Casual Sales Are Tax-Exempt

If you have a garage sale in your neighborhood, you do not need to collect sales taxes. But if you regularly sell antiques out of your house to your neighbors, you are running a business. Casual sales do not take place more than twice a year.

Computers May Be Tax-Exempt

In some states, computers and accessories used in your business operations are tax-exempt. However, the computers must be used directly to manufacture finished goods. Technology companies can especially benefit from this. Ask your accountant to verify this before claiming this exemption.

EMERSON'S experience

Your business may be considered tax-exempt based on its location. In Pennsylvania, where I live, Opportunity Zones, for example, eliminate certain taxes for businesses that locate in qualified areas. To find these programs, check with your county or look on your state's website for community and economic development.

Internet Entrepreneurs Pay Sales Tax Too

You only charge sales taxes when you ship a product to a state where you have a physical presence or license to do business.

Some Services May Be Tax-Exempt

Ask your accountant to clarify your state's sales tax code. Every state has a list of services that are taxable. If your business service is not listed, breathe easy: Your company is tax-exempt.

EMERSON'S action steps

1. Consult with a small business lawyer about establishing your legal entity.
2. Seek out an accountant who works with small businesses and has experience in your industry.
3. Make sure you understand the specific sales tax requirements in your state.
4. Stay on top of your tax liabilities. Entrepreneurs are always susceptible to an audit by the IRS.

PART II
Get Set!

CHAPTER 8

WHO IS YOUR TARGET CUSTOMER?

Most entrepreneurs start with marketing tactics. That's understandable. We are all bombarded with marketing messages all day every day, so it seems easy to do marketing—but it's not. A recent Gartner study reported that the average small business owner is exposed to as many as four thousand marketing messages a week and retains three or four of them. It's exciting to think about what you want to call your restaurant and how awesome the grand opening event will be, but before you go there—stop and think.

- Who is your target customer?
- Who are you going to serve?
- Will you target by gender, geographic area, or age?
- What is your customer's occupation?

- Is she college educated?
- How often will she dine with you?
- How much disposable income does she have?
- Is she a soccer mom or a single urbanite in her late twenties?
- What will work for her on your menu?
- Is she a health-conscious person who is anti-carbs or a pulled pork–eating meat lover?

Before you figure out how you will go to market, determine if there *is* a market.

This chapter on marketing appears right before the chapter on developing a business plan on purpose. Before you go through the exercise of writing a business plan, you must figure out whether or not you have a paying customer, because if you can't identify your niche target customer, that's an indication that you might have a half-baked business idea.

Your marketing plan is the foundation upon which your business plan is built. A solid marketing plan includes everything from defining the market opportunity, clarifying your products or core services, identifying your niche target customer, and developing the value proposition, to analyzing threats, developing your marketing strategy, key messaging, pricing strategy, tactics, and defining your marketing budget. Why is it so detailed? It is much easier and cheaper to do your homework on your target customer before you open your doors rather than scramble to get a handle on that after the business is operating. A good marketing plan forces you to set SMART goals based on the sales you want to generate. More on this later. First, let's define some basic marketing terms.

- **Marketing.** Marketing is anything you do to generate sales—the activities that create brand awareness that a product or service exists. Marketing presents products or services in ways that make them desirable.

- **Branding.** What is a brand? It is the image or culture you create for your product or service. Your company's brand is defined largely by its brand identity, which includes the company's name, logo, product and packaging design, your brand voice, and everything visual about your business. Your brand includes direct customer interaction, as well as how you engage with your social media followers, fans, connections, and prospects. Your brand identity is how you communicate.

- **Advertising.** This is a tactic of marketing. It's an openly sponsored, nonpersonal message that promotes or sells a product, service, or idea. Paid ads draw attention to products or services in order to build awareness and generate sales.

- **Market Research.** Market research is about collecting information that provides insight into your customers' thinking, buying patterns, and location. Market research can also assist you to monitor market trends. This data helps you decide how to reach customers and influences your advertising approach.

- **Competitive Analysis.** Competitive analysis identifies your competitors and evaluates their marketing strategies to determine their strengths and weaknesses relative to those of your own product or service.

- **Value Proposition.** Also known as unique selling proposition, your value proposition is your competitive advantage or key benefits of your product or service. It clearly articulates why someone should want to buy from you.

- **Sales.** This refers to the delivery of a product or service for a cost.

- **Profit.** Profit is the difference between the amount of revenue earned and the amount spent on buying, operating, providing, or manufacturing a product or service. From the start, you need to make sure you are making enough profit on every sale to stay in business.

EMERSON'S essentials

Marketing strategy is about creating value for your customer that is not easily duplicable by your competition.

Your Marketing Mix

In order to build an effective marketing plan it helps to have a framework. The four Ps of marketing are a set of marketing tools that small businesses use to pursue their marketing objectives. The four Ps concept was introduced in 1960 by E. Jerome McCarthy in his book *Basic Marketing: A Managerial Approach*. The four Ps are regarded as the pillars of marketing strategy. Here's an explanation of each of the four Ps of marketing:

1. **Product:** Describes the product or service you will offer, including branding, size, options, quality, warranties, and packaging. Key specifics that you need to define include how the product or service will meet client needs, what geographic area will be served, the features and benefits, your value proposition, and how the product or offering will be manufactured or performed.

2. **Placement:** Describes how a product goes from factory to the physical location, gets priced, and is ready for the customers to buy. You'll need to clarify how a product or service will be sold or delivered; distribution channels can include brick-and-mortar stores, online stores and marketplaces (Amazon, Etsy, eBay), virtual service distribution, direct mail, catalogs, sales reps, affiliates, referrals, wholesalers, distributors, and direct sales advertising that will be leveraged to make your product or service available for purchase.

3. **Promotion:** Outlines what marketing channels you'll use to get the word out about your product or service, including website, content, speaking, direct mail, books, telemarketing, radio, magazines, industry publications, public relations, infomercials, and advertising strategy (TV/cable ads, radio ads, online ads, social ads, marketplace ads, retargeting, SMS/text ads, voice marketing, etc.).

4. **Price:** This is where you determine what the market will pay. Based on positioning, decide whether your product or service will have premium or discount pricing. Pricing strategy is all about pricing your product or service for your different target markets. Determine the list price, discounts, wholesale allowances, markdowns, payment periods, and credit terms.

In the 1990s, marketing strategy shifted from being about mass marketing to being customer-centric. Robert F. Lauterborn developed the four Cs marketing model that focuses on niche marketing that is especially relevant to today's digital-savvy consumer. He believed that businesses should only sell products that customers want. The four Cs concept is not just about marketing and selling a product; it's also about communicating with the niche target customer from the beginning of the process as you build the ideal solution to the customer's problem. The four Cs of marketing model is about creating a quality buying experience for your target customer at both the point of sale and after the sale in order to drive profit, repeat orders, and gain competitive advantage. Professor Lauterborn's four Cs are customer, cost, communication, and convenience. Each replaces one of the four Ps:

1. **Customer:** *Customer replaces Product.* The first C focuses on what the customer wants and needs. Instead of focusing on the product itself, customer feedback will drive your decision-making process.

Once you understand your customer, it becomes much easier to create a product that will benefit them. But you must consider how you are going to determine what your customer wants.

2. **Cost:** *Cost replaces Price.* Cost in this context reflects the total cost of ownership, i.e., disposables, installation, implementation, etc. Price is only one aspect of cost to a customer. It may include things such as the time and gas to get to a retail store to make a purchase, or shipping cost when you order a product online. You must think about the cost to satisfy the customer. Too often business owners believe that price drives a purchasing decision. Positioning is far more important than price because it reflects perceived value. Price can be used as a positioning vehicle to deliver results against the competition.

3. **Communication:** *Communication replaces Promotion.* As a business owner you must intimately understand the needs and wants of your target customer as you are designing the solution. Communication includes any form of engagement including online and traditional advertising, public relations, content, social media, email, or any other communications between you and your prospective buyer. Your goal must be to build an authentic, meaningful brand that resonates with your target customer. Like the effort you put into social media, it's about give-to-get between you and your target customer.

4. **Convenience:** *Convenience replaces Place.* Convenience focuses on the ease of buying a product or service, including finding the product or service as well as finding information about the product or service. Today's customers have too many choices and demand convenience. You must understand how your target market prefers to buy and adapt as needed. You must also build frictionless buying experiences that delight your niche target customer.

In 2017, yet another marketing thought leader said that since the marketplace is now digital as much as it is physical, the four Cs required another look. Marketing consultant Jake Rector wrote that it was time to look at a new digital marketing model for the twenty-first century. So he updated the four Cs, also as they relate to the original four Ps, to be more relevant to today's marketplace. His four Cs are choice, convenience, cross-device, and creative:

1. **Choice:** *Choice replaces Product.* Customers have an endless supply of choices. Brands must meet consumer demand with highly relevant and personalized products and services and promotional campaigns.

2. **Convenience:** *Convenience replaces Price.* When your customer buys something, they want it now. Price is secondary to convenience. Speed of delivery is the deciding factor on how and when purchases are made. This category is still about creating amazing customer experiences though, which is why free shipping remains an attractive perk.

3. **Cross-Device:** *Cross-Device replaces Place.* Marketing is now omni-channel across all devices and points of sale. Brands must create mutually rewarding, connected experiences across online and offline channels. Your customer uses multiple devices throughout the day, and your brand experience must be seamless across every customer touchpoint too. Brands must deliver relevant marketing messages and opportunities to buy anytime, anywhere, on any screen.

4. **Creative:** *Creative replaces Promotion.* Your target customer is hit with hundreds of ads and marketing messages daily. Creative storytelling is the solution to break through the noise and get your brand noticed. Sales funnels are a perfect example of this. (More on this in Chapter 13: How to Develop a Sales Process.)

From brand awareness to nurture sequences and sales conversion, creative storytelling allows brands to deliver tailored messaging to their customer depending on where they are in the buyer journey. Conversion requires multiple touch points. Business owners have to find the right order in which to tell their brand's story to engage and build trust with the target customer.

Each of these versions of marketing theory includes nuggets that are still relevant to today's marketplace. Taken together, they should enable you to build a layered approach to your marketing strategy for your new business to engage the 24/7 connected customer.

EMERSON'S essentials

We are in the age of the customer. Offering an excellent customer experience is necessary to even be in the game. Nobody falls in love with just okay.

Here are a few things you should know before you develop your marketing plan:

Much of the information you need to learn about your target customers is free or low cost. Spend time on social media listening to your potential customers; learn your industry keywords and hashtags to track social conversations and your competition. You can also reach out to your local business librarian for help with market research, grab a 10K report from a business-to-business (B2B) target, read industry websites and publications, read government publications, and talk to potential customers. These are all great sources of information.

The Next Step

Your marketing plan brings together your understanding of the market, your customer, your competition, and your pricing. From these, it generates a strategic and tactical approach to marketing your product or service. Your plan will also need to delineate your positioning in the marketplace, your niche focus, value proposition, and competitive advantage. In other words, your marketing plan clarifies who your customer is and why he should buy from you. Now that you understand the four Ps and the four Cs, you need to start building your marketing plan. Here are some other elements to consider for the plan:

- Validate the market.
- Develop your customer persona.
- Create your value proposition.
- Conduct competitive analysis.

Validate the Market

One of the most important aspects of starting a business is validating that there will be customers willing to pay for your product or service. There is nothing more frustrating than spending your time, energy, and resources building a product that you think people will love, only to find out that no one is interested. So how do you validate the market?

- **Talk to potential customers.** Leverage your network and reach out to people who are likely your ideal customer. Start with your friends and family and then branch out to social media connections for one-on-one conversations. This is a great way to learn how to serve your potential niche or even develop different versions and pricing for your product.
- **Make a few sales.** If you have customers willing to pay you, that's a good indication you might have a real business.

- **Evaluate the current market.** Competition is a good thing; that means there is a customer base. Competitive research can help you see who is already in the marketplace and look for gaps in the market that might be a great niche to pursue.
- **Research existing demand.** The easiest way to understand customer demand is to analyze search volume. Go to Google Trends. This is a free tool that allows you to see how often people are searching for a product or service. Google's Keyword Planner tool allows you to search for keywords and phrases related to your product or service. Knowing how many people are searching and what they are searching for can help you make a more informed decision about whether to pursue this business.
- **Conduct a survey.** Once you have an idea of who you might want to target for business, conduct an anonymous survey of people who are not related to you to get honest feedback.
- **Launch a crowdfunding campaign.** If you have a product-based business, launching a crowdfunding campaign can do a few things for you: (1) gauge customer interest, (2) raise funds to build inventory, and (3) create a per-order customer base. (There's more about crowdfunding best practices in Chapter 10.)

EMERSON'S essentials

There is room for everyone to find a customer base. Think about a shoe store: How many different kinds of shoes do they sell? Exactly. There is a shoe for every kind of shoe lover. There is room for everyone to build a niche audience, as long as you have a quality product, relevant message, and savvy marketing.

Develop a Customer Persona

Customer personas are fictitious models of an ideal customer based on data and market research. They take into account income, geographic location, age, gender, education, marital status, profession, etc. You should be able to see the face of your customer as you design a solution. Remember, the better you know your customer, the better your chances of making the sale. Keep in mind that your competition is targeting the same people you are, and your message can easily get lost in advertising clutter and spam. So developing a story that will resonate with the ideal customer is key.

Create Your Value Proposition

Your value proposition is the core of your competitive advantage as a small business. The most compelling value propositions are concise, highlight quantifiable outcomes, and clearly distinguish the value the seller is offering compared to that of the competition. Customers may overlook your products and services if you don't know how to communicate why they should come to you and not your competitors, but be careful as you craft this message, as it's not a simple tagline on your website's header. Many small business owners set themselves up for failure by never genuinely articulating a compelling value proposition. You must establish a substantive, unique value proposition if you want to go from idea to successful business.

Start by identifying what qualities your customers value most and least about your service. You must build your value proposition on customers' perceptions of your product's value to them. This approach is called WII-FM, or What's in It for Me? Draw customers in with your benefit statements, demonstrate your product/service with video and content, and close the sale with your unique value proposition. Stay true to your core principles and train your staff to keep your brand promise, and your business will stand out. No company is born with a value proposition. You must create, nurture, and propagate it if you want to reap the benefits.

Conduct Competitive Analysis

Competitive analysis is an essential part of building your marketing plan. You need to identify your competitors and determine how you plan to deal with them. While analyzing your competition, you should not be trying to steal their ideas; instead, you want to understand their strengths, weaknesses, pricing, and customer service gaps so that you can build your company's unique value proposition.

Look at Public Records

Companies that are publicly held are required to file 10K reports with the Securities and Exchange Commission (SEC), and these reports are available on the company's website under investor relations. The reports are required to list company vulnerabilities, so they can be very valuable to you. It is also a good idea to do some research at the Patent and Trademark Office website to see if your competitors have filed anything that indicates they are developing a new product or service.

Attend Industry Conferences

A great way to learn about your competitors and what they offer is by attending professional conferences and trade shows. You can walk up to their booth and grab a sales kit. You could also build a relationship with your top competitor, and they just might share helpful information. You'll never know until you ask.

Review Their Website and SEO Strategy

You should also visit your competitors' websites to see what they are promoting, sign up for their newsletters, and use some tech tools to get some insight into their keywords and how they are using paid advertising such as Google Ads.

Other Resources

Here are two other valuable sources of information about your potential competitors:

- SpyFu is one of my favorite Internet tools. It can provide insight into your competitor's keywords and any Google Ads they are buying.
- You can also set Google Alerts on your top keywords and on your top three competitors. Be sure to set one on your name and the name of your company to track who is talking about you.

Track Social Media Marketing Efforts

When it comes to social media there are a few things that you should note about your competition: What platforms do they use? What hashtags do they use? What type of content do they create or share? How often? How many followers, friends, or connections do they have? Do they use social media for customer service, and if so, what is their response time?

Track Content Strategy

Every brand uses some form of content to generate leads and generate brand awareness with target customers. The content is used on their website and on social media. Most businesses also have a visual marketing strategy as well. You want to observe how competitors use content to unify their brand story. Specifically, you'll want to look at the content type and quality, how it is shared, frequency of publication, repurpose strategy, and the target audience.

Types of content include blog posts, podcasts, infographics, webinars, quotes, photos, custom graphics, live video, checklists, ebooks, cheat sheets, Instagram posts, TikTok videos, Pinterest boards, quiz marketing, vlogs (video interviews), product demonstration videos, reviews, newsletters, Twitter chats, and Q&A interviews.

Review Email Strategy

Sign up for your competitor's newsletter on their website or download their free offer to get on their email list. You want to track how often they send emails, any sales offers, and see if they include images or mixed media or are mobile optimized.

Do a Mystery Shopping Exercise

Get an intern or someone who doesn't have an email that will trace back to your company to call up your top competitors pretending to be a lead looking for a sales pitch. You want to see their sales materials, especially their pitch slide deck. Study their sales processes and delivery systems. How can you improve on them and make your customer's experience better?

Success leaves clues everywhere. Be sure to review your top competitors on a regular basis. You could get inspired to develop your next innovation.

EMERSON'S essentials

If you can't identify a competitive advantage or value proposition, that's a good indication that you need to come up with another business idea.

Niche Marketing

Selecting the right niche target customer is key to long-term business success. It will help you determine which marketing channels to use to engage your target audience. Customers have high expectations and, thanks to technology, instant access to all kinds of information and competitive pricing. It's essential to develop your marketing plan to attract a specific niche target customer straight out of the gate, otherwise you could waste a lot of time and money.

A niche is a particular market or specialty area where a company finds it profitable to concentrate its efforts. Niche marketing offers a concentration of clients in an area of limited competition.

A market niche can be a specific geographic area such as the Mid-Atlantic region, a specialty industry such as sugar-free desserts, an ethnic or age group such as millennials, or any other group of people with certain common characteristics (for example, people who do not own cars). Niche businesses can position themselves as specialists, charge more, and generate higher profit margins.

Find Your Dream Niche

A niche can be anywhere, including under your nose or online. Sometimes a niche is something no one else does (a CPA friend of mine specializes in real estate accounting), or sometimes it's something no one else wants to do (picking up dog poop, a small business that generates $100,000 per year). Sometimes a niche can be created by improving a common product already on the market (e.g., Stevia, a natural sugar substitute that is extracted from a plant native to South America). A business that focuses on addressing an unmet need can be a niche business too. Lefty's, a California-based retail store, sells school supplies, kitchen goods, gardening tools, and more for lefties. Ten percent of the population is left-handed, so this is a great niche to pursue.

Your task is finding, or inventing, your niche. Here are some general guidelines:

- **Go with what you know.** Bob spent many years in the tow truck business. He was located close to a major turnpike, and the work was very competitive. In an effort to find a niche, he decided to buy a tow truck that could handle big rigs. There were no competitors within fifty miles, and his revenues rose 50 percent the first year. He was an expert in towing and used his skills to specialize.

- **Look for "you must be kidding" opportunities.** The enterprising entrepreneur can find a pot of gold in everything from septic maintenance services and bat removal to window washing and pet sitting. Typically, if you pursue an "ugly" business you can bet that the competitors will be few and the potential unlimited.

- **Turn a hobby into a money machine.** Stories abound about makers who went from the kitchen to national enterprises because they were tuned in to America's taste buds. Michael Davidson, CEO of Black Infusions, is one such business owner. When he launched his artisanal spirits collection that includes gold apricot vodka, he was inspired by a personal interest in wine making and the desire to create a spirit that pairs well with food. His brand promise is that he sells only great-tasting, all-natural products that are free of artificial sugars and preservatives of any kind.

- **Invent something.** Mother Necessity is always looking for solutions to problems. Ped Egg, Jet Ski, plastic garbage bags, and WD-40 are just a few of the many products created by inventors who made a niche where none had existed before. If you can create an improvement that the public can embrace, congratulations, you might have a great niche business.

EMERSON'S experience

I have a friend who worked for a major multinational corporation early in his career. As a product manager, he saw an opportunity for his business to expand their services into a product area that would generate an additional $25 million in revenue a year.

He researched the market, developed the business plan, and presented the business case to his superiors. In the end, the company passed on the opportunity, claiming that $25 million in revenue was not significant enough to dedicate the resources to pursue the opportunity. My friend realized that if they didn't want to pursue it, he could. He worked for that business another nine months to build up capital, then quit to start his firm. He has not hit $25 million yet, but he is closing in on it.

Define SMART Goals

What are your marketing goals for the coming twelve months? It's got to be more than "I want customers." Instead, make your goals SMART:

- Specific
- Measurable
- Attainable
- Realistic
- Timely

It's important to utilize this SMART framework when you define your marketing goals.

EMERSON'S essentials

Once you flesh out your invention, confirm customer interest, and develop a prototype, you'll need to protect your idea before you partner with a manufacturer. Patents are your legal protection against anyone else stealing your idea. The two most common types are design patent and utility patent. If you decide to pursue a utility patent you should start with a provisional patent, which is essentially a low-cost method of protecting your idea for a period of one year while you test your product and market. After a year, you can choose to pursue the full utility patent or trash the idea.

Make Them Tough

Setting attainable goals is a bit of a balancing act: You don't want them to be so easy that you achieve them quickly and don't continue to push the envelope, but if they're too lofty then you're setting yourself up for stress and failure.

Stay Relevant

If your goals aren't directly relevant to building your brand and closing sales then you're wasting your time and resources.

Put an End Date on Your Goals

How will you measure your progress? Invest at least six months in any new marketing tactic, as that should give you enough time to start to see results.

Here are a few sample SMART goals:

- Grow website traffic by 30 percent in twelve months
- Increase sales by 15 percent in twelve months
- Gain 100 Facebook followers in three months

Your marketing strategy must answer why specific tactics make sense for your brand. Your marketing should be ahead of the market and not be reactionary to your competitors. On a sheet of paper, make a list of your SMART goals and refer to it often.

When approaching a new marketing niche, it's important to be clear about the benefit you are offering, and to speak the language of your customer. Are you talking to high school principals, nurses, landscapers, or HVAC retailers? They all have different issues and communicate using a lot of industry-specific language. In other words, you need to sound like your market and be prepared to communicate with them as an insider.

Testing Your Niche

Before settling on your niche, test it to make sure a business aimed at it will be viable. There are several ways you can do this:

- If a real niche exists, chances are you'll find media targeting it. Look for blogs, magazines, trade journals, influencers, and other media aimed at your customer base.
- Find a strategic partner or blogger who already has a relationship with your target audience and offer to barter or pay them for a dedicated email blast or a newsletter blurb offer with an embedded trace link to see if their audience is interested in your offer.
- Run low-cost online ads on platforms such as Facebook, Google, or YouTube for a couple weeks to test public interest in your product. If you get a good response, follow up with a survey to get more information on who is buying your product.
- Rent a mailing list. Business associations and niche-specific publications will sometimes rent you their mailing lists for a one-time use fee. If you rent a set of names, do not attempt to reuse the list. Pub-

lications always place trace names in the list that will alert them to any violation of the usage terms. You can usually sort the names on the list by variables such as zip code, gender, income, etc. Contact a list broker or a direct mail house in your area or online.

EMERSON'S essentials

If everyone can use your product or service, no one will. Be known for something. People respect expert knowledge. The more you know, the better your expertise, and the stronger your chances of success.

Now that you've decided on your niche, you can begin to get into the details of how you will market to your customers. In the next chapter, we'll develop the business plan, and you'll see how getting clear about marketing will set you up to make all the other business decisions to come.

EMERSON'S action steps

Your marketing plan is the lifeblood of your business; that's why you need to develop it before the business plan.

1. Identify the four Ps and the four Cs that are relevant to your new business.
2. Do the necessary market research.
3. Study the competition.
4. Identify your niche target customer.
5. Develop a detailed customer persona.
6. Develop a marketing strategy that will deliver your niche target customer.

CHAPTER 9

EVERY BUSINESS NEEDS A PLAN

Morris Anderson, a business expert, said, "A ship without a compass will have a tough time navigating." For the same reason, any small business, whether it has a million-dollar launch or just a few hundred dollars to get started, needs a business plan. It does not have to be complex; it can be as minimal as ten pages or as long as forty or so. What counts is the quality of the strategy outlined in those pages. Strategy is about competition. How are you going to position your business in the marketplace and create a value proposition that is not easily duplicable by your competition? Whether you start a small lawn-care service or a major manufacturing firm with one hundred employees, your plan needs to identify a niche customer and be well researched and have reasonable sales projections.

Writing a business plan is a good exercise. It will force you to describe the fundamental elements of your business: what business you are in, why you are in it, how big the market opportunity is, and what the growth potential is in your market. The plan must also describe the availability of skilled labor necessary to meet your company needs, and how you will generate additional start-up capital. It will help you think through how you will actually run your business. If you follow the twelve-month planning process laid out in this book, you will accomplish the following:

- Establish a clear connection between your business strategy and your marketing plan
- Define the latest socioeconomic data and industry trends
- Develop a clear rationale for the marketing strategy
- Highlight the experience and management skills of the business owner(s)
- Produce a capacity-building plan to accommodate growing operations
- Develop an operating budget and realistic sales projections

There are three main uses for a business plan: communication, management, and planning.

1. As a communication tool, the business plan helps the owner:
   - Attract investment capital
   - Secure loans
   - Attract employees
   - Attract strategic business partners
   - Demonstrate profitability
   - Demonstrate due diligence

2. As a management tool, the business plan helps the owner:
   - Track, monitor, and evaluate progress

- Modify strategy as knowledge and experience are gained
- Establish timelines and milestones
- Compare sales projections to actual accomplishments

3. As a planning tool, the business plan helps the owner:
   - Advance through the phases of business development
   - Identify roadblocks and obstacles
   - Establish alternative plans

EMERSON'S essentials

People spend more time planning their vacation than they do planning how to run their small business. The business plan is your road map to get you from where you are to where you want to be as a business owner.

What's in a Business Plan?

The components of the plan include:

- Cover Page
- Executive Summary
- Business Description
- Market Analysis
- Marketing Plan
- Operations Plan
- Management Team
- Intellectual Property Strategy
- Financial Projections

Cover Page

This first page of the business plan should include the date, name of the business, names of all business owners, and contact information for the key person. The cover page should also be marked confidential. Your plan is private, and you should not show it to just anyone. It contains information about your strategies, tactics, and projected revenues. Be careful how widely you circulate it.

Executive Summary

This should be written after the document is complete. The executive summary gives an overview of the important aspects of your business. It provides a brief description of the product or service and generates interest in your business idea. It clarifies the size of the market opportunity, communicates your marketing strategy, and explains your unique selling position in the marketplace. It summarizes how much money you will need to start or grow, and estimates your year-over-year expected profitability. It should include a paragraph or two on each section of the business plan. It should not be more than two pages.

Business Description

This is the explanation of your business idea. It should be brief, well thought out, and easy to understand. Fortunately, you've already done a lot of this thinking while you made your life plan, clarified your business concept, and drew up your marketing plan. Now you can bring all that thinking together in this document. Make sure not to include any proprietary information about your business.

Your business description needs to answers these questions:

- What is your product or set of core business services?
- What is your unique value proposition?
- What is your business strategy or competitive advantage?

- How will your product or service meet the needs of your customers?
- What are your product development milestones?

Market Analysis

Market analysis starts with a market summary outlining every potential customer segment. Then it drills down to how much each customer segment is worth. You must determine which segment your business will focus on as a main revenue target. The marketing strategy outlines the marketing approach for your target segment.

Generally, you'll have a greater chance of success if you pursue a business in a growing industry. If you are not in a growth industry you need to understand how long you can keep your business going before the market moves or is saturated. Will you serve an unmet need in the market? How will you solve your customer's pain? Be exhaustive about your competitive research. You want to understand how often and under what conditions the customer buys the product or service, and then figure out how to get them to buy it from you. Prying a customer from an existing vendor is no small challenge.

Marketing Plan

Chapter 8 reviewed in some detail the elements of a marketing plan and why it is so critical in the development of your business. It is essential to know who's buying and why they should buy from you. By building customer personas, you will be able to identify and prioritize changes to your marketing messaging based on what your customers need the most. If you cannot "see" the face of the customer, there is no use in even finishing the business plan.

Are you selling hot dogs and sandwiches on a busy college campus? Your student-customer marketing is clear. Will you specialize in quality shirts for big and tall men? Or will you look at serving the needs of new moms? You need a specific niche customer and unique value proposition.

In either case, you will have to give a reason for those customers to purchase from your company. You want to take a forward-looking approach to branding your business. It can positively influence your positioning in the eyes of your target customer, which is directly connected to how much they will value your product or service and be willing to pay.

Positioning also directs the marketing approach. Whether it is providing "the highest-quality beef hot dogs at the lowest price" or offering "the widest range of sizes in high-quality men's shirts," think about how to brand position your product.

How the brand is positioned becomes the reason why a customer picks you over your competitor. Your marketing plan should convey to anyone reading your business plan what you see as your brand positioning, value proposition, and competitive advantage. You also need to explain your cost/pricing strategy, competitive analysis, communications approach, distribution channels, and creative/promotion strategy, packing, sales process, and much more.

If you are targeting consumers directly, it's important to understand the types of potential consumer audiences that you can attract to create your niche. You might start with an entire generation of customers then get more specific:

- Female baby boomer widows still living in their own home
- Married Generation Xers with children
- Male millennials who live in urban centers and enjoy a healthy lifestyle
- Generation Z females with significant student loan debt who aspire to start a business

Operations Plan

This explains how you plan to run the business on a day-to-day level. Managing your enterprise is serious work. As the boss, you need to orchestrate how the business will run while keeping costs down and maximizing profits. You need to have a clear process for delivery of your product or service, including inventory, materials management, storage, project management, software needs, staffing, fulfillment, handling customer complaints, shipping and receiving, and much more.

If you are manufacturing a product, it is important to establish how you will track all the raw materials, processes, finished goods, and shipped goods. You must know how you will handle the many emergencies, large and small, that will arise. Your business plan should include as much detail as possible so anyone can see how you expect things to work.

Running your business can be as simple as going to a big-box retailer and stocking up on more hot dogs, rolls, condiments, napkins, soda, etc. for that week's business of running a hot dog stand. Or, it can be as complicated as contracting with a foreign manufacturer to create luxury shirts, getting payment to the manufacturer up front, getting your finished goods through customs, price-tagging them for wholesale and retail, stocking the store, scheduling staff, promotions, and much more.

Other issues that fall under operations include location, business permits, inventory management, electricity, insurance requirements, and communications needs. If you have construction needs to fit out your space or licensing and zoning requirements to adhere to, any of these areas can stop you from opening your doors and should be addressed as a detailed part of your business plan. This section should touch on personnel issues like payroll cash flow needs, required skill sets, training, and total headcount, as they have a direct impact on your operations plan, your sales projections, and your business budget.

Management Team

Highlighting your expertise and background is critical to giving your new business credibility. Your knowledge of your industry and your relationships with potential strategic partners and customers will be an important asset to your business. As your business grows and your management team takes shape, any new team members should have business experiences, significant business/sales contacts, demonstrated leadership, and/or technical savvy. Your business plan must explain what sort of management team you will put together. (Of course, if you're the only one involved in the business, this doesn't apply.)

Intellectual Property Strategy

Once you develop a concept or a product that you want to introduce into the marketplace, you should consider whether that idea is subject to intellectual property protections. Intellectual property (IP) refers to creations of the mind, such as inventions; literary and artistic works; designs; and symbols, names, and images used in commerce. There are four types of intellectual property protections: copyrights, patents, trademarks, and trade secrets. You may need to file a patent application or register a copyright to protect your idea if you are using a special trade name or a symbol associated with your business name; this will keep competitors from using your brand name or hashtag.

Seek the advice of an intellectual property attorney. If you choose to register your intellectual property yourself, you'll need to understand a few basic concepts to determine what kinds of protections are available for your original ideas and concepts.

Trademarks/Trade Names

A trademark (™) is a distinctive sign or symbol used by a business to identify to consumers the source of its products and services. A trademark will distinguish your products or services from those of other businesses. A trademark can be a name, word, phrase, hashtag, symbol, logo, design, image, or a combination of these. For instance, if you are fan of the NBC series *Law & Order*, you may know that legendary music producer Mike

Post copyrighted the "chong, chong" music that introduces scenes in the show, and he makes a royalty every time it's played on TV.

The owner of a registered trademark can bring a lawsuit for trademark infringement to prevent the unauthorized use of that trademark. However, you're not required to register your trademark. The owner of an unregistered trademark may also file suit for infringement, but the trademark can only be protected within the geographical area in which it has been used.

Trade Secrets

A trade secret is a special formula, process, design, pattern, practice, or compilation of information used by a business to gain a competitive advantage. For example, the secret formula for making Coca-Cola is a protected trade secret. The method you use for doing business, your customer lists, your client files…these are all trade secrets.

A business owner need not register trade secrets to secure protection. Instead, you must ensure that your employees understand they are under a duty of confidentiality not to disclose any trade secrets. Consider having them sign a nondisclosure, noncompete agreement when you hire them that clearly states how confidential business information is to be handled. Your attorney can draw up this document for you.

Copyrights

The creator of an original work, such as a song, book, film, or software package, is entitled to exclusive use rights under copyright laws. If you have an employee write a computer program to run software on your business systems, you are entitled to copyright protection to keep other businesses from copying your computer software. This will allow you as the business owner to exploit the financial value of any original works prepared by you or your employees. Any original work your employees create while on the clock becomes the intellectual property of your business.

As the copyright holder, you have the right to copy the work, make adaptations, and sell or license the right to use the copyrighted works to other businesses and individuals. To obtain this protection, the original work need only be fixed in a tangible medium such as a writing or a recording, or saved in a file format. It's a good idea for business owners to obtain a formal copyright registration with the United States Copyright Office in Washington, DC. It is inexpensive and provides peace of mind and the necessary documentation in case you need to file a copyright infringement suit against a competitor. Another reason to research copyright protection is so that you don't unknowingly violate someone else's copyrighted material.

EMERSON'S essentials

There is no such thing as the poor man's copyright protection. Please do not think that you have copyright protection by mailing yourself a copy of your work in a sealed envelope.

Patents

If you have developed a product that does something no other product does, you need to obtain a patent. This applies to any new and useful process, machine, method, or design. Your patent application will have to describe claims concerning your invention in some detail, to show what is unique about it. A good patent lawyer can help you prepare an application and submit it to the United States Patent and Trademark Office.

Intellectual Property Checklist

Use this checklist to decide whether you need to protect any of your business ideas and products.

❏ Is your product/service unique?

❏ Is your production process unique?

❏ Are you using a specialized process or formula that could be patented?

To find a reliable intellectual property lawyer, ask for a referral from another business lawyer. You can also use Rocket Lawyer or Nolo, both of which offer lawyer referrals. Keep in mind investors will want to know if your product or service can be or is protected. Good legal advice is valuable beyond measure when it comes to intellectual property. As soon as you can, engage a patent or copyright lawyer who has experience with small business owners.

Financial Projections

The financial projections lay out your operational budget and sales projections for your business. Typically, the first thing any investor, lender, or bank will want to know is how much money your business will generate and by when. You will need to create a tight, well thought-out, realistic budget plan that includes the amount of personal financial risk you are willing to take. If you are not comfortable with accounting, you should engage an accountant or a seasoned bookkeeper to help you pull together your initial financial projections.

EMERSON'S essentials

You should use up-to-date financial statements to make informed business decisions. It is a good idea to work alongside your accountant for a while to learn the financial inner workings of your business. Using business plan software and business planning books will make developing your financial plan a lot easier.

Your financial plan is your best estimate of your company's financial future. It is only an estimate because you have no idea how your company will perform until you have operated for six months to a year. Your plan should include a one-year operating budget and up to three years of company sales projections.

EMERSON'S essentials

When it comes to developing sales projections, be conservative and realistic. Know your numbers, and be able to defend them. The worst thing you can do is to develop financial projections that don't make sense, particularly if you plan to pursue funding.

Your plan should also include a break-even analysis. The process of developing your financial projections will help you understand how many sales must be generated to cover your expenses and eventually earn the company a profit.

Good financial projections include the following information:

- Projected manufacturing costs (i.e., what it will cost to make your product or provide your service)
- Projected operating expenses (e.g., office rental, supplies, payroll, etc.)
- Salaries (including what you will pay yourself and what you will pay your employees)
- Freelance/contract employee expenses
- Start-up costs
- Marketing expenses
- Professional services (legal and accounting support)
- Projected business taxes
- Projected revenue, broken down by product line and source

Certain expenses, such as some of your start-up costs, can be amortized over the first twelve months you're in operation.

The Best Way to Write a Business Plan

The easiest thing to do is use business plan software. You'll find several options, but one of the best is at www.liveplan.com. This walks you step-by-step through each area, including financial projections. There are also many books available that will help you write your business plan. Two of the best are *Lean Business Planning* by Tim Berry and *The Successful Business Plan* by Rhonda Abrams. The latter includes spreadsheet templates and is a helpful reference guide. You can also hire a consultant to write your business plan. This option may sound attractive, but since you have all the information the consultant will be using, it's more cost-effective to do it yourself. Keep in mind that the cost of hiring a consultant can range from $1,500–$7,500.

Finally, consider taking a business plan course at a local community college, small business development center (SBDC), or nonprofit organization that provides technical assistance to small businesses in your area. Fees for such courses can run from $75–$2,500, but it will be money well spent. I also offer a ten-week online course, Become Your Own Boss, which walks you through this book in depth and helps you develop a complete business plan. You can sign up at www.smallbizladyuniversity.com.

Think about your business plan as a living and breathing document that should be reviewed and updated every six months to make sure your business is on the right track.

EMERSON'S action steps

1. Understand the three main uses for a business plan: communication, management, and planning.
2. Validate your business model and build the case for why your business will be successful.
3. Sign up for business plan software.
4. Have an intellectual property protection strategy.
5. Work with your accountant to develop an operating budget and sales projections.
6. Check out my Become Your Own Boss course to complete your business plan at www.smallbizladyuniversity.com.

CHAPTER 10

GET YOUR FINANCING TOGETHER

Businesses run on money, and profit is how we keep score in business. You'll have to keep that reality in the front of your thoughts every day as you run your business.

To get the business going, you'll need money for your start-up costs. This chapter discusses finding the money to build your entrepreneurial dream and how to manage it once your business is operating. Which option you choose to finance your business depends on your situation and how much risk you are able and willing to bear.

Savings

Your savings account is one of the best ways to finance your new business venture. If you have followed the advice in Chapter 4, you have spent time trimming your spending habits and accumulating personal funds that you can access. Keep in mind, you shouldn't put at risk your emergency funds.

You can, of course, take money directly out of your savings account and spend it on start-up costs. But it's also possible to leave your money in savings or a money market account, letting it continue to earn interest, and instead use it as leverage to get the cash you need.

For example, if you purchase CDs—certificates of deposit—you can use them as collateral for a loan. You will earn interest on the CD (usually from 1–3 percent), which lowers the cost of the loan. Talk about a win/win!

The benefits of this approach are:

- This is a great way to borrow if you have less than stellar credit, and it keeps your borrowing costs low.
- Because you are borrowing against your own money, there is no need to convince a banker to believe in your plan—you believe in yourself and put your own money behind it.
- It's quick. You can usually leave your old job sooner if you have the financing for your new business in place, allowing you to focus 100 percent of your time on the business.
- By buying brokered CDs you can shop for the best from banks around the country. CDs are federally insured up to $100,000, so it doesn't matter where you purchase them.

Drawbacks to this approach include:

- If you default on your loan, you risk losing all of your money invested in the CDs.

- Using personal funds as collateral ties up the money, preventing you from using it in other ways.
- Interest rates can change and go higher.

Balancing advantages against drawbacks, this is one of the best ways to borrow money for your business. You have maximum flexibility and freedom to operate. At the same time, as with all methods of raising start-up funds, you must decide how big a risk you're willing to take.

Your Retirement Fund

Now could be the time to borrow against your 401(k) in order to finance your life's dream. Overall, this is a great source of borrowing, assuming you are in a position to keep your job during the twelve months prior to starting your business. For that year, you will continue to put money into your account. If your company matches the funds you put into the account, so much the better.

Borrowing against your 401(k) allows you to use your own money and then pay it back to yourself.

EMERSON'S essentials

Pay yourself from your business's profits. As your business begins to make money, plan to pay back the money you took to fund its start-up from your retirement account or savings. Put that cost in your budget, so you stick to it.

The benefits of this approach include:

- You can usually borrow up to 50 percent of the vested balance of your retirement account, or $50,000, whichever is less.

- Assuming you make interest payments on time, you will pay little or no taxes or penalties.
- The interest you are paying is going back into your account, not to the bank.

The drawbacks of borrowing against your retirement account include:

- Most plans have a five-year repayment cycle. If you leave your job before the loan is repaid, it will become due within a short time after you announce that you are leaving your company.
- You can only borrow against your 401(k) if you have your job. But if you become a victim of corporate downsizing, after taking the loan, you must repay the loan within thirty to ninety days to avoid heavy taxes and penalties.
- There are heavy tax penalties if you touch your 401(k) or IRA money if you are under fifty-nine-and-a-half years of age.
- There can be fees or maintenance charges to borrow the funds. Discuss your 401(k) account with your financial planner—or your company's human resources representative (although you don't need to tell them that you're planning to use the funds for start-up costs for your business).

In general, you should discuss your plan with your financial planner or accountant before borrowing any money from your 401(k). If you are over fifty and nearing the age for retirement, you may not want to use this source to fund your business. It's not a good idea to mortgage your future retirement to start your business when there are other ways of getting seed capital.

Home Equity Line of Credit

This was once the most common way to fund a business. Since the Great Recession of 2007–2009, it has become less popular. All things considered though, this can be a great way to fund your business, assuming you have substantial equity in your home.

You should not borrow more than 80 percent of your home's value, and if you go beyond 80 percent your lender will probably require you to buy private mortgage insurance (PMI).

Having a golden credit score is your best asset in obtaining any financing for your business, but especially when you are securing a home equity loan. It could allow you to keep your borrowing costs down and stretch out the payment schedule from five to twenty years.

A home equity line of credit (HELOC) generally carries a variable interest rate. Current interest rates and the condition of the borrowing market are the biggest factors in your decision on this type of financing. The markets usually change in waves, but if you have a low interest rate on your first mortgage, keep it and look at a HELOC. If you have a high interest rate relative to the current market, first consider refinancing. This will put you in the best borrowing position.

The benefits of this approach include:

- You can access the funds quickly and easily. If you already have an established HELOC you can just write a check against the line of credit. If you don't, opening a home equity line of credit is a relatively simple procedure.
- There are options to ensure you get the lowest interest rate possible.

Drawbacks include:

- Using home equity means you are using your house as collateral. Never forget this. If your business fails and you cannot repay the loan, the bank can foreclose on your home.
- The overall housing market can affect your ability to get this type of loan.

■ HELOC interest rates are adjustable and may rise higher than other sources.

■ A new loan against your home will require an appraisal of your home. This can be a problem if the housing market has been in decline and houses in your area have lost value.

■ If you borrow too much and the house loses value, you could wind up owing more than the house is worth. The collapse of the housing market in the 2008 recession eroded equity, and many business owners lost their homes and their businesses when banks liquidated the collateral when the loan payments could not be met. If you pursue a bank loan with an SBA guarantee, pledging your home as collateral is often required to secure the loan. Taking the risk is tempting, but beware of the cost if things go wrong.

Friends and Family

This can be the best or worst source of money for starting a business. Family members often can lend you the funding you need, but repayment terms can cause a rift in the family.

Sometimes family members will want a piece of the business in exchange for the loan. Others might believe their loan gives them license to freely advise you on the best way to run your business. None of this makes for a happy business owner. But if you need funding and a friend or family member is willing to lend it to you, you may need to suck it up for your dream. You can tolerate anything for a little while.

The positive side of borrowing from friends and family is that they're in the best position to understand your passion for your business. Many successful small businesses have been started with loans from parents, friends, or in-laws.

Your best option is to find a family member who is reasonable to deal with and happy to be a silent partner. Be sure to agree on reasonable borrowing terms that include interest payments. Consult your lawyer or accountant for guidance.

Although you're borrowing from someone you know, perhaps intimately, still document the agreement in writing so everyone is clear on the terms should any problems arise. Look online for a sample loan agreement or have an attorney draw up a contract that everyone can sign.

Bank Loans

Typically, banks do not give loans to start-up businesses. There are SBA 7(a) loans and some franchises that facilitate and assist with start-up funding, but most often bank loans are only an option if you have been in business for two to three years. You need to show your bank a positive track record, including growing revenues, strong cash flow management, and good personal credit profiles of all the owners. You may need to sign a personal guarantee and provide your spouse as a cosigner in order to qualify for a loan. Many national bank chains cannot adequately service the needs of small businesses. Smaller banks move faster in terms of processing the loan, but they can be much more rigid in their requirements. Also, loan decisions are not made locally at national bank chains, so the business banker you have a relationship with may have limited influence over your loan decision. Smaller banks can be more flexible, and you will usually be dealing with a local decision-maker.

To sum up how a bank will examine your application, keep in mind the six Cs:

1. **Capacity:** What's your ability to repay the loan? This is the single most important factor your bank will consider in deciding whether to advance you money. Your cash flow statement in your financial plan will provide the answer. A good cash flow statement details your ability to repay the loan in a timely manner.

2. **Credit:** What is your personal credit score? Banks will require you to sign a personal guarantee on a loan to share the risk. The higher your credit score, the more favorable terms you can negotiate.

3. **Capital:** How much money do you need and how will you use those funds? The more money you ask for, the more scrutiny your loan application will receive. Educate yourself about the types and amounts of loans your bank will typically approve.

4. **Collateral:** What assets can you provide as security for your loan? These could include your house, car, or business assets, particularly if you have expensive equipment (trucks, industrial printers, broadcast video cameras, etc.). Collateral greatly increases your chances of getting a loan. Beware, however, of lenders that over-collateralize loans. Watch for phrases in your loan papers like "We will take a business lien on all current and future business assets." That is a steep price to pay for a $35,000 loan.

5. **Character:** How good is your reputation? Who knows you? Are you trustworthy? Smaller local banks will look at this aspect closely. As well, all banks will look at your business experience and your industry background.

6. **Conditions:** What are your loan's terms and conditions? Is it a good deal for you or the lender? Your bank wants to make sure that you are using the loan for a legitimate business purpose. Some lenders will require invoices from your vendors and will cut checks directly to the vendors for payment.

SBA microloans can be secured through credit unions, community development financial institutions (CDFIs), and nonprofit organizations that support small businesses. Such organizations typically give SBA-backed microloans of $10,000–$35,000, but once you build a repayment history you can go after a higher dollar amount with any traditional lending institution.

The SBA 7(a) loan can be another option for start-ups, but you need a tight business plan and excellent personal credit to even be considered. Funding decisions can take time, but these government-backed loans aim to help small businesses without sufficient external funding sources to get running. The SBA does not loan money directly; they simply guarantee a percentage of a loan made through traditional banks, credit unions, CDFIs, and some alternative lenders.

It's possible that you may not want to borrow the money to cover your start-up costs, either because you have only a fair credit rating or because you have a low tolerance for risk, and borrowing always involves some risk. Therefore, rather than borrowing the money, you might consider getting outside investors.

Angel Investors

Many people have a lot of money and are willing to help others who have ideas and energy. Angel investors are interested in making money, but they do not need or want daily interaction with the business.

Unlike venture capitalists (discussed later in this chapter), such investors don't typically demand management control, financial control, or payback within three to five years. Angels will often serve as senior advisors or board members for your business, but they rarely want to be involved in the direct management of the company.

Angel investors usually will fund lower-growth-rate projects or smaller business ideas than venture capitalists. They are also more tolerant of high-risk businesses than are venture capitalists. For some, it is not just about the money—they want to give back. Many of them thrive on the energy new entrepreneurs radiate.

An investor is different from a lender. Angel investors will generally become your business partners, and in return for their investment capital they will want a substantial amount of equity in the business.

EMERSON'S essentials

Angel investment can make your business soar—but only if your idea is strong. One of the most famous cases of an angel investor was when Sun Microsystems founder Andy Bechtolsheim wrote out a check for $100,000 to Larry Page and Sergey Brin to start a business manufacturing and selling search engine software. Page and Brin decided to call their company Google. And we know how that ended up!

Often it can take up to two years to secure angel funding. Angels are looking for talent first and great ideas second. And they can come from lots of different places:

- **Friends and family.** Your uncle or aunt or next-door neighbor may not be willing to lend you money to start your business. They might, however, want to invest and take a small equity stake in the business if they believe in you and your idea. The key difference between loans and investments is that loans have repayment terms; investors are along for the ride and willing to risk their capital.
- **Local retired businesspeople.** Often, wealthy retirees want to give something back to their community. If you are starting a local business that will clearly benefit your neighborhood, you may seem like a good investment opportunity.
- **Organizations.** Sometimes angels gather in groups so they can pool their resources and expand their funding. For example, the New Orleans Startup Fund is a nonprofit venture fund focused on growing the business innovation engine in the Greater New Orleans region. The fund exists to boost the ecosystem of early-stage businesses looking for capital.

Your success in reaching angel investors and convincing them to back your business will depend heavily on your skills delivering your pitch (also known as your "elevator pitch"). Angels want business owners who are working hard to develop their ideas, who can articulate their product, vision, and target market, and who have the management skills to lead a successful business.

EMERSON'S essentials

You must have a strong elevator pitch about your business. Practice this in front of a mirror, to your spouse, to your friends, or to anyone else who will listen. Pare it down so you've got the essentials of your business in a strong, compelling, and brief presentation. You should be able to deliver this pitch in thirty to sixty seconds at most—the time you spend riding in an elevator with someone.

Venture Capitalists (VCs) or Private Equity Investors

Venture capitalists are looking for business ventures that will grow fast and be bought by other, larger companies at a significant profit to stockholders, or that will let investors cash out in three to five years at a significant rate of return (typically 30–100 percent). Venture capitalist firms, also known as private equity firms, typically manage their investments like stock portfolios or pension funds, betting that a few investments will hit it big in order to fund all of the ones that do not make it. They are not passive investors and will want to see a detailed business plan with financial projections, with an eye toward accelerated growth.

Lining up venture capital is not a quick process and can take even longer than getting backing from an angel investor.

VCs will typically take a controlling stake (meaning controlling ownership) in the firm, hold financial control of the business (meaning check-writing authority), and eventually will bring in their own management team to ensure that the business is run in a manner consistent with their growth objectives. Sensitive entrepreneurs, beware. If you're used to calling all the shots, VCs can be pushy and hard to work with. They monitor business progress regularly and demand that management make decisions in the investors' best interests.

An investment agreement drawn up by venture capitalists will include milestones you must reach, usually measured by financial metrics such as revenue growth, profitability, etc. If you fail to meet these milestones, the VCs will gain increased control of the business.

The good thing about venture capitalists is that they have money and the management experience that many small business owners lack. They also have insight and access to connections that could make the difference between being a huge success and losing everything. This is the most expensive capital in the marketplace, but in some cases it is the only viable option. For a directory of venture capital firms and angel investors, check out www.vfinance.com.

Crowdfunding

Crowdfunding is when you raise funds for a project or business by soliciting contributions from a large number of people via the Internet. A key element of successful crowdfunding is to have an extensive network before you launch your campaign. You also need to invest in a great video that turns your business into a cause. Then you go out to your network and to strangers, mainly through social media and email, to raise capital.

Crowdfunding offers individual business owners a chance to showcase their businesses and projects to the entire world of potential investors, and build a client base. There are more than two thousand active crowdfunding websites worldwide; some of the biggest are Kickstarter, GoFundMe, and Indiegogo.

Each site offers a unique spin in terms of the types of projects and businesses they like to feature, but they all basically operate in the same way. These sites will take a commission fee of 5–9 percent of what you raise, but there's no limit on how much you can raise.

EMERSON'S essentials

The beauty of crowdfunding is that the focus is not on what you do; people will support you because of why you do it. If you can tell a great story about your "why," people will give you money because they believe in your idea.

If you are going to use a crowdfunding platform, you'll need to create a profile with a written description of the project, a short video, and a list of rewards you are willing to give in exchange for a donation. You must also decide on a funding goal and a time frame. You can choose up to sixty days to achieve your goal. But choose your financial goal carefully and conservatively, because some sites only pay if your goal is reached. If your goal is $5,000 and you raise $4,999.00 in donations—you get nothing and the pledges are returned.

Fans of crowdfunding say it's a resource model that unlocks the ability for people to launch their dream business, people who have not been able to raise capital because they have been shut out of traditional investor networks.

Why Support Crowdfunding Campaigns?

There are four main reasons people will support your crowdfunding initiative:

1. They connect with your cause.
2. They want one of your rewards.
3. They want your product.
4. They love your video about your product or cause.

EMERSON'S essentials

One of the biggest challenges I see with crowdfunding is the misconception that if you build it, they will come. You can't just build a crowdfunding campaign and wait for it to go viral. You must have a separate marketing plan just for your crowdfunding campaign, and crowdfunding projects require a significant amount of public relations effort before, during, and after the campaign. Should you be using that time just trying to secure customers?

If you decide to develop a crowdfunding campaign to launch your business idea, research which sites are right for your type of business. Once you decide on the right crowdfunding site, follow these five steps to build your campaign profile:

1. **Work your network first.** Be active on social media at least six months before the launch of your campaign. If you can't get people you know to invest in your idea, no one else will. About a third of your early pledges will come from your personal network.

2. **Tell a good story.** If you have a strong idea, tell a compelling story about it. Clarify your business goals and highlight your team if you have one.

3. **Do not exaggerate.** Be enthusiastic about your business idea, but make sure you do not overhype your project. If you promise

things you cannot deliver, it will turn into a PR, and potentially legal, nightmare.

4. **Have great rewards.** People love to get something, even if it's small, for their donation, so be creative. Dinner with the creators of the project or VIP tickets to a special event are good examples of rewards.

5. **Donor relations are critical.** PR nightmares and lawsuits can happen if you can't deliver your product when you promised. Have a plan to communicate with your network and your donors after the funding campaign is over. You want to keep the people who donate engaged and excited, because you may need to raise more money in the future.

Things to Remember

There are some important points to keep in mind if you decide to use crowdfunding as a source of financing:

- Don't let the crowdfunding campaign take over your business. It will take a huge effort to be successful with your crowdfunding campaign, and your main business operations will suffer as a result. Don't lose sight of what is in the best interest of your business, regardless of what it takes to market your crowdfunding campaign.

- Take the time to find a good manufacturing partner. When you do things in a rush, you don't get the best deal. Start researching and interviewing manufacturers and vendors before your campaign starts so that you can keep your delivery date to donors.

- Don't be afraid to miss your campaign delivery date. It's not ideal to miss your delivery date, but you don't want to put out a product that will destroy your brand. Take the time to tweak your product so that it's what you promised. Just communicate with donors beforehand about potential delays.

■ Keep your funders informed. You need to communicate what's going on. Rewards don't pan out sometimes. You might have manufacturing issues and might miss your delivery deadline; just keep your funders informed. They believe in your cause, and if your communication is timely they will be more understanding.

Crowdfunding is a great opportunity to raise funds for a new business, build a base of loyal customers, or expand the product line of an existing business. Think of it as a marketing and funding platform, where you can build a customer base before you even launch your business. But, keep in mind that the real work begins after the funds come through. When you raise money through crowdfunding, the money must be used for what you say it's going to be used for, and products and rewards need to be delivered in the time frame as promised. Resist the urge to exaggerate your timelines and deliverables. There have been cases where people have run fraudulent campaigns, and lawsuits from donors resulted. The platform can pursue you to get money back. Don't risk your business reputation this way.

Next Steps

Once you get donor funds and/or business revenues, you'll need to build good money management processes. One of the keys to cash management is being on top of your monthly financial statements. By the fifteenth of every month, you should have a current balance sheet, profit and loss statement (P&L), and a statement of cash flows. These will tell you what your business did in terms of revenue and expenses for the previous month. Your bookkeeper or accounting clerk should produce these three financial statements for you each month. Falling behind in this paperwork is very dangerous to the health of your business.

EMERSON'S essentials

You need accurate financial information to make good business decisions. You must know how much each job or product costs you and what your profit margin was on that particular job or product. You also need up-to-date financial information so that you can effectively track your COGS (cost of goods sold).

So you don't get lost amid all the jargon, here are some basic definitions for you to keep in mind as your business proceeds:

- Cash flow statement is cash receipts minus cash payments from a given period.
- Balance sheet is a statement showing your company's financial position at the end of an accounting period.
- Income statement is your company's net income for the accounting period; also called a profit and loss statement, or P&L.
- Cost of goods sold (COGS) is the figure representing the cost of buying raw materials and producing finished goods.

In addition to the financial statements, you must track your expenses against your budget. All the trouble you went to in drawing up that budget in your business plan will be wasted if you don't keep to it.

In the fourth quarter of each year, you should prepare a budget and make sales projections for the next year. When preparing the budget, it is important to review your prior year's projections versus your actual expenses. This information will help you create a more accurate budget and assist you in reducing any out-of-control expenses.

Unless you are a sole proprietorship, business taxes are due by March 15 of every year, not in April like personal income taxes. Some business owners strategically delay paying business taxes until October. Talk with your accountant about whether you should file for an extension.

EMERSON'S action steps

1. Determine the amount of money you will need to start your business.
2. Draw up a list of possible sources for the money.
3. Evaluate the amount of risk you are willing to take.
4. If you are considering borrowing against your 401(k) account, remember that you must hold on to your current job until the loan is paid off.
5. Make a list of local angel investors who might be interested in your business idea.
6. Compile a list of possible venture capitalists to pitch in your area.
7. Consider if you have the bandwidth to take on a crowdfunding campaign.
8. Have your accountant provide monthly financial statements so that you'll be able to make business decisions based on up-to-date financial information.

CHAPTER 11

DEVELOP YOUR WEBSITE

Once you name your business and get your business plan and financing in order, it's time to build your business assets. Your first concern should be building your website. Your website is your number one sales tool. *Ninety-three percent of online experiences begin with a search engine.* People will Google your business before they ever call you for information or a quote. In fact, 81 percent of people do some type of online research before making a large purchase. People go online to make connections, gather information, and be entertained. They also go online to do product research, shop, stay informed, and share their experiences (good or bad) with others. Building a helpful business website will go a long way toward building trust with your target customer.

143

Designing Your Website Strategy

When it comes to designing a website, you have six options: You can build a traditional small business website, a portfolio website, a blog, a personal brand website, an e-commerce website, or a membership website. The best option depends on what kind of business you run.

EMERSON'S experience

Think about building your brand online as a four-legged stool. The first leg is your website, which is the most valuable real estate you own in marketing. The second leg is content marketing, which is how you demonstrate your expertise through how-to videos, newsletters, blog articles, podcasts, images, custom graphics, quotes, live video streaming, infographics, product reviews, Q&A interviews, voice-activated content, live chat, chatbots, etc. The third leg is social media, which is how you engage directly with your target customers and share your content on social media platforms. The fourth leg is email marketing, which is how you build a relationship and trust with potential customers. You must have two to three ways to attract visitors to give you their contact information and email address when they arrive on your website. Then you use your email marketing software to send a series of emails to your prospective customers; this is known as a nurture sequence. These emails are designed to introduce you and your brand and drive the potential customer down your buyer journey. Hopefully you'll turn them into a customer within ninety days of getting their email address.

Traditional Website

A traditional small business website is purely informational, featuring store hours, locations, menu, services, and contact information. This type of site doesn't feature a shopping cart, as it's really a brochure-type site that provides a description of services and contact information. You also want to make sure there's a click-to-call feature on this type of site for mobile web users.

Portfolio Website

A portfolio website is ideal to market personal services directly to potential clients. This kind of website often features a portfolio of work, software to schedule a consultation, or a public calendar to automate booking an appointment and securing a deposit. This is a great option for service businesses such as photographers, graphic designers, makeup artists, cake decorators, etc. When it's easy for potential customers to see your work and read or watch testimonials, you can get hired quickly.

Blog Website

A blog website is perfect for professional service businesses and experts who want to demonstrate their expertise. My goal at https://succeedasyourownboss.com, a blog website, is to educate small business owners on how to start or grow a business. I also encourage people to hire me as a business coach, download ebooks, order my books, or enroll in one of my online courses. I use content to build my brand on social media and sell my products and services. If you launch a blog website, you must update the content two or three times a week to gain a loyal following.

Personal Brand Website

A personal brand website is popular with business owners who want to become a brand or influencer. Most people just show hero pictures of themselves in action on stage, or they might use video. They can share a demo reel of media appearances or a cut from a keynote speech. They might feature book covers, a media kit, a headshot, a bio, a list of signature topics, sample interview questions, and testimonials. This website is mainly used to build authority and social proof with potential customers.

E-commerce Website

E-commerce websites are strictly for selling products. You'll need great pictures of your products as well as titles and descriptions with strong keywords. Then you need to decide on a shopping cart system, a payment processor, and a shipping partner. All of these decisions are simplified if you use an e-commerce platform builder. (More on this in Chapter 14: Selling Online.)

Membership Website

A membership site allows you to put specialized content behind a paywall. You can build this kind of site with a plug-in on the WordPress platform. A membership site is a very popular online business model. Major money can be made from offering online courses, premium VIP forums, and webinars. Users register and sign up for your subscription service to see your private content. Some membership websites offer a free introductory membership for seven to thirty days, and then the paid membership kicks in. There are many other possible options as well. You can offer a 2–5 percent discount for an annual payment, or you can offer recurring monthly subscriptions that automatically renew. You also want to make sure there's a community aspect to this type of site where members can easily share it. Often members want to network with each other. Some of the plug-ins to consider include Paid Memberships Pro, Paid Member Subscriptions, and WishList Member.

EMERSON'S experience

The membership site www.socialsaleslink.com charges members $29 a month for premium membership for information on how to use LinkedIn for social selling. They do demonstrations on LinkedIn Sales Navigator and also offer live coaching weekly. With a thousand-plus members, the site rakes in more than $30,000 a month.

Other Considerations

Once you've decided on what type of website you will have, you can take a shortcut and use a website builder service to create your initial website; popular options include Squarespace, Web.com, and Weebly. If you are building an e-commerce site, popular options include Shopify, BigCommerce, and Wix. These plug and play services will allow you to create a quick drag and drop website, but be aware that some of these sites scream newbie start-up business unless you customize the templates.

There are a variety of questions you need to answer before you get started building your website. Specifically, you'll want to address the following six issues:

1. **Your market position.** Are you going to be known for selection and delivery? If so, your website must be fast and have a great selection. Your design, in other words, must reflect the qualities you want your customers to associate with your business.

2. **Your degree of customization.** Your website should provide a customized solution for your target customers based on survey data and highlight the benefits that you provide. Let's say you target pet owners. You can create a website all about dogs. Or, you can develop a niche website that specializes in a specific breed.

3. **Your architecture.** The architectural design of the website will convey the credibility of the site. A website design that looks bad gives the impression that your company is not technologically advanced or isn't willing to invest in its appearance.

4. **Your navigation.** Good websites are easy to use. No one likes a website where you need to search for how to place an order, how to contact the company, or how to pay. Not only should all the links on your pages work; they should also be easy to find, be fast, and direct.

5. **Your expertise.** The best way to demonstrate your expertise is with a blog. The quality of content on your website is important. Serious websites are updated two or three times a week minimum. Do keyword research to help you know the right headlines and meta tags to use to develop relevant content that will show up in online searches and satisfy your prospect's search intent.

6. **Your trustworthiness.** You want your website to be perceived as trustworthy. Make sure your contact information can be easily found and that it includes a street address, a phone number, and an email address that someone checks. Having no contact information may lead visitors to question the legitimacy of your business.

You also want to make sure your website is mobile optimized for a smartphone or a tablet device.

1. **Use a Responsive Theme.** The site will adjust to whatever kind of device accesses the URL.

2. **Prioritize Speed.** Speed is everything when marketing online. People want things even faster on a mobile device.

3. **Simplify Your Navigation.** Mobile screens are smaller than laptops. Design your navigation bar with minimal information.

4. **Keep Opt-In Forms Short.** Name, email, and cellphone number is all you need. Asking visitors for too much information will turn off mobile visitors.

If you are going to build an e-commerce site, post your return policy and any guarantees that you offer. Also consider joining the Better Business Bureau (BBB) and adding their logo to your site along with all the payment types you accept (e.g., PayPal, Visa, American Express, Mastercard, Google Pay, Apple Pay, and Discover). Post testimonials and five-star Yelp ratings. Note: Video testimonials are the best kind.

EMERSON'S essentials

Don't build a website that is just a sales page; make sure you build a website that is an actual resource to your target customer. This is true even if you are an e-commerce business.

Building Your Website

There are two ways to make a website: with a website builder or with WordPress. Website builders are perfect for the non–tech savvy; they have everything you need to create a website. You can drag and drop images, videos, new pages, contact forms, and everything else, without having to code. You need a little more technical skill for WordPress. WordPress is not an all-in-one package. It's a content management system (CMS) that allows you to create and organize digital content.

Whether you choose a website builder or WordPress, you'll need to arrange for web hosting and domain registration separately.

Secure a Web Domain Name

A good domain name is one that is memorable or that relates to something in which visitors are interested. If you can include a keyword in your web address, that's all the better for search engine optimization (SEO). SEO web design is a way of designing a website to make it search engine–friendly. You want to make a website SEO-friendly so that Google can crawl each page, interpret the content, and index it in its database. All of this is designed to drive organic search traffic to your site. Your goal is to develop content that lands your brand on the first page of a Google search, which makes it much easier to get found by potential customers.

Purchase at least two versions of your web domain name (.com, .net, .tv, .name, .store, or .info). There are many companies available online that you can use to register a domain name. Among the largest are:

- www.domain.com
- www.dreamhost.com
- www.bluehost.com
- www.namecheap.com
- www.hostgator.com

Don't ask your web designer to register the name for you; do it yourself. That way, you'll control your web/URL address. Purchasing a domain name generally will cost between $14 and $35, if you include private registration. Paying this fee entitles you to use the name for a year, with the option to reregister it annually. Selecting a URL can be a time-consuming process, as so many domain names have already been taken. Be careful not to use a word that is hard to spell or that you are spelling in an unusual way. The goal is to be found by your customers.

Select a Web Hosting Company

A web hosting company provides server space for your website. When it comes to selecting a hosting company, it's all about speed, security, and support. Hosting services range in prices from $15 a month to a few hundred dollars a month, depending on what you need. When you are just getting started you can consider a cloud-based option (such as Amazon Web Services or Microsoft Azure), or a virtual private server (VPS). A VPS gives you dedicated resources, more flexibility as you grow, greater security and improved speed, and there is a managed service. Managed hosting is when a hosting company handles the setup, administration, management, and support of a server for a small business website.

Your hosting package should also include your email addresses. You want to make sure you have enough space not only to build your current website, but also to expand in the future as your company grows. You also want to make sure your website can handle a sudden surge of traffic should your product be featured in the media as one of Oprah's Favorite Things one holiday.

When selecting your web hosting provider, ask these questions:

- How many customers do they serve?
- How secure is the site? What type of protection do they offer?
- How fast will they guarantee they can get your site up if it crashes?
- How often do they back up the sites they host?
- How much storage do they provide? (100 MB is a good starting point.)
- Will the hosting package also support a blog?
- What are the setup and monthly fees?
- How many email addresses come with the package?
- When is technical support available?

Check Out the Competition Online

You need to know who is out there in the global marketplace. Look at the features and functionality of your competition's websites. Take note of what you like and don't like. If you plan to sell your products online, make sure to examine as many online stores as possible. Take note of the layout and functionality and the software for their shopping cart. Consider buying something to really map their shopping cart experience and fulfillment processes. I recommend SpyFu .com and Alexa.com to look at the traffic and websites of your competitors.

Develop a Website Architecture

Think through how you want your website to look and function. One of the simplest ways to develop a website architecture is to use a

PowerPoint slide template for an organizational chart. Start with the home page at the top and list the navigation and other pages underneath.

Develop Website Copy

No matter whom you hire to build your website, not much can be done until you create some content for the web pages. Before you start developing the content, you need to learn keywords and phrases people might use to find your business in an online search. We'll discuss keywords and content development in Chapter 12: How to Become a Social Media Activist.

Your basic pages include:

- **About Us:** Information on your company history, whom you serve, and your mission statement.
- **Our Team or Our Founder:** Mini bios of company managers with headshots, or just the company founder.
- **Our Services:** A list of services available with calendar links to schedule an initial consultation; depending on your industry, you can charge for the initial consultation.
- **Store:** A list of products with images and links to buy.
- **Contact Us:** Make sure there's an email address, a business address, and a phone number listed, not just a blank form to fill out.

Typically, you should put no more than 250 words on a web page. After looking at the competitor sites, draft the initial content for your website. Make sure you have someone copyedit all website copy for typos and grammar mistakes. Nothing is more unprofessional than typos on your website.

Hire a Professional

Unless you are an experienced web developer, leave it to an expert. No matter how well you know the vendor, draw up a formal contract, with a strict timeline and progression payments. Use a work-for-hire contract that clearly says you own the finished website. There is a difference between graphic design and web development. Make sure your vendor has experience designing websites that convert to sales.

EMERSON'S experience

When I first developed my original website, I hired some friends to develop it. I let them register the site domain for me as well as create the artwork and functionality. I knew these people extremely well and had no concerns about their work or professionalism. Rather than draw up a contract, we made a verbal agreement, and I paid them all the money up front. These were big mistakes!

I nearly went to court over my website after they claimed ownership of my domain name. I was dissatisfied with the site they built and wanted to move on to another vendor, and they refused to release the passwords to my site. Luckily, I had filed a trademark for my name and slogan. My lawyer was able to negotiate control of my site from the hosting company, but only after a lot of back and forth and legal expenses. You will find in business, there are plenty of opportunities to learn lessons; some are more expensive than others.

Create a Request for Proposal (RFP)

To make sure that you create the website you really want, you'll need to create a request for proposal for potential vendors.

If you are just getting started, build a WordPress site so that you will be able to add pages and make text changes yourself. Get at least three quotes. Good ways to find website vendors are by asking other business owners for referrals. Then look for vendors on upwork.com, fivrr.com, 99designs, or LinkedIn. Put out the word to your social media connections for referrals.

Your vendor should have a portfolio of websites to review. Require at least three references and call them. Attach your site architecture to the RFP so your potential vendor is clear on how much work is involved in building your website.

Learn the Basics

Do your homework and learn the basics of WordPress. You must learn how to add a page; change text; add graphics and photos; and use meta tags, alt tags, and hyperlinks. You also need to understand the administration of your site and what your hosting package provides. Keep your admin passwords to access the site in a safe place and learn how to add and delete email addresses. It is best to start learning this stuff as your site is being built, so you can ask your web developer technical questions. You can also learn basics by watching YouTube videos or taking a class online. This is especially important if you don't have enough money to hire someone to help you maintain the site once it's built.

Use Educational Resources

If educational resources are offered by your new hosting platform, be sure to take advantage of them to get up to speed quickly. Most hosting services offer training videos or slideshows for new users.

Select a Payment Processor

If you want to sell your products or services directly from your website, you'll need a payment processor to take credit cards on your website. PayPal is an option, but you can also use Square or Stripe. In addition, many of the accounting software providers offer credit card processing directly as well. Do your homework and shop around for the best rates. You will pay a charge per transaction.

Select a Shopping Cart System

Your shopping cart system works in tandem with your payment processing. The right shopping cart makes it easy to buy from you. After all, you want to make it as easy as possible for customers to give you their money and receive their merchandise or service.

Like everything else on the web, a shopping cart system is just software. Once the customer hits the submit button in your store, back-end mechanisms kick into gear to send funds to your account (minus the credit card fees). The shopping cart will send a thank-you confirmation email to the buyer with their digital receipt and/or one to you that signals you or your fulfillment house to mail the customer their merchandise. Make sure you use a shopping cart that can connect to shipping software, such as ShipStation.

Monetizing Your Website

The biggest benefit of bringing a lot of traffic to your website is that you can turn your traffic into money. Here are four strategies to turn your website traffic into a cash machine:

Sell Your Own Products

You should sell your own products and services with a store on your website. But you can sell with content too. Now, there's a right way and a wrong way to go about this. The wrong way is to write a super-promotional post about your product. That's the fast track to turning off your blog readers. The right way is to provide value in that copy about your product. Write a post on ten unique ways to solve a problem and mention your product as one option. Include a video on your site's landing page of a customer demonstrating your product or giving a testimonial. Include a call to action (CTA) in your post to buy. You can add a link or a pop-up exit graphic to remind them about your offer. This should entice visitors to click and buy.

Sponsored Posts

Let's say you write a small business blog, and a well-known office supply company wants access to your loyal readers. You could charge them to publish a sponsored blog post. Depending on the size of your traffic, you can charge a significant fee to write a post for your site. The company can give you the post, or you can write a post about their products yourself. (Always charge an additional fee if you write the post.) The clients should get a link or two back to their website within the article. This strategy also works really well if you have a significant social media following to boost the views of the post.

Affiliate Links

You can also become an affiliate for brands you admire. You place links to these products on your more popular posts, or you draft a post to specifically promote their product. Then, whenever anyone clicks on the link and makes a purchase, the affiliate pays you a commission.

You can work one-on-one with companies that offer affiliate programs, or you can use a network like ShareASale or ClickBank and handpick the brands you want to represent on your blog.

Advertising

Finally, you can accept advertising on your website. This works best once your traffic is pretty high (meaning more than twenty thousand unique visitors a month), since advertisers want to maximize the number of people who see their ad. Typically, websites that offer ads have several sizes to choose from, including a wide banner up at the top and smaller square ads on the sidebar. You can offer video roll-ins and price these accordingly. You have two options for finding advertisers:

1. Include a link on your site that advertisers can click to sign up with you.
2. Work through an ad network like AdMob or Outbrain that automates ad placements for your website.

You will, of course, have greater earning potential with the first option, but you'll need to do more legwork to find advertisers. With an ad network you can specify the types of ads you want, install some code, and let that network do the work for you.

Make sure you set aside budget to update your website every year. It's the best place to sell yourself and your business. Update your content often, and focus on creating value for your target audience.

EMERSON'S action steps

1. Research whether your desired website URL is available and purchase it immediately.
2. Thoroughly research web hosting and online shopping carts before deciding on vendors.
3. Develop your navigation in an org chart and create an RFP for your website.
4. Hire a professional to build your website.
5. Be sure to use a work-for-hire contract and spell out a timeline.
6. Never pay all up front for web development.

CHAPTER 12

How to Become a
Social Media Activist

Now that we reviewed developing a website, it's time to discuss building your content and social media marketing strategy. Without content, there's nothing to share on social media sites, so let's start there.

Can any small business benefit from content marketing? Absolutely, YES! According to the Content Marketing Institute (CMI), 91 percent of business-to-business (B2B) marketers use content marketing to reach customers. Eighty-six percent of business-to-consumer (B2C) businesses think content marketing is a key strategy. Content marketing is the best way to create a steady stream of inbound leads for your small business. If you develop compelling content and share it regularly through social media, your niche target customer will find you. If you want to build your brand online, my best advice is to start developing relevant content that your target customers want and need to consume.

Your content must solve problems for your target customers, and educate, enlighten, or entertain them. Developing compelling content is hard, but if you want to be regarded as an expert in your field you need to demonstrate your expertise to your audience, and developing content is the best way to accomplish that goal. You can't have lunch or coffee with every prospect. Sharing content through social media is a way to reach the masses and draw them to you.

EMERSON'S essentials

Before you start to develop any content, you need a content strategy. In fact, your content strategy should be an essential part of your marketing strategy.

Content marketing is a lot of work. You really need to know your customer: what their struggles are, where they spend time online, and how they like to interact with content. Then, you must build a great website, populate it with valuable content on a regular schedule, and leverage social media to share the content to draw in target customers. You also need to make an irresistible offer on your landing page to get them to join your email list or to make a sale. It's rare that someone will buy the first time they interact with your content. So, you'll need to follow up with an email to build trust.

Content Strategy versus Content Marketing

Content strategy is the method by which you determine what kind of content you will develop and where you will share it across social media to build your online brand. Content marketing is how you promote the content you are creating and publishing on a consistent basis. Your goal is to engage with a specific target audience. Then leverage social media to join online conversations with your niche target customers. As potential customers express concerns, ask questions, or seek recommendations, you'll use your social media presence and content to position your brand as a resource. Quality content is currency online. Here are five big reasons why you should start developing content:

1. **To generate sales:** Regularly updated content gives people a reason to visit your website. From there, they are just one click away from discovering your products and services.

2. **To get found online:** Valuable content boosts SEO (search engine optimization), which generates a higher number of search matches and increases your organic search rankings with Google.

3. **To build your social media credibility:** If you share quality content with your followers and connections across social media, it's a great way to deliver value to your target audience and demonstrate your expertise.

4. **To establish your thought leadership:** If you are an expert in your field, what better way to show it off than to write or record compelling content that helps your audience understand their biggest challenges and how you can solve their problems?

5. **To generate opportunities:** Publishing great content can lead to more than just sales. People who read your content might invite you to be a speaker, appear on a podcast, write a book, write for a major media organization, or even appear on TV as an expert.

EMERSON'S experience

Your quality content will give you access to new relationships, events, and conversations. I was invited to write a regular column for *Entrepreneur* magazine, and two years later I was given a column in *The New York Times' You're the Boss* blog, both thanks to the strength and reputation of my own blog at https://succeedasyourownboss.com. My editor at *Entrepreneur* said she read my blog for a year before contacting me about writing for her publication. When you demonstrate your expertise well, you don't have to sell. You also do not have to explain how you can solve your customer's problem—because she already sees you as a resource. That's why developing your own signature content is so powerful.

Once you have a content strategy in place, you can stay consistent with content development by using an editorial calendar to plan your content in advance. Storytelling is a major component of a successful content strategy. Sharing personal stories builds trust with the audience. Use your content to build relationships and tell stories that allow your target audience to feel like you are just like them. Have some fun with your content too. Sharing your personality is a way to attract potential customers who want to get to know you.

Twenty Great Content Marketing Ideas

Here are some new ideas for developing content; it's a mix of direct content ideas, apps, audio and voice marketing, and social media tips for any type of business:

1. **How-to advice/checklists:** People are always searching online for information about how to do something. If you provide a

how-to blog post or a checklist to help your audience get started quickly, you could become the top authority in your industry.

2. **Product reviews:** Your target audience could be hungry for details on what's hot right now—writing or recording product reviews are perfect for this.

3. **Interviews:** You can gain credibility by being associated with other notable people. Reach out to authors/experts in your field to conduct an interview. This is a perfect podcast, video, or blog post.

4. **Branded YouTube channel:** If you hate to write, launch a video series of short-form how-to videos. You can record them with your smartphone, a small HD digital video camera, or use your laptop to record via Facebook Live, Zoom, or Google Meet. Just make sure you invest in a quality tripod, good lighting, and a professional microphone.

5. **Live Q&A videos:** Use live video via Facebook, Instagram, LinkedIn, TikTok, or Twitter to answer questions for potential clients. You can also turn customer questions into written blog posts. Many people could use the information.

6. **Newsletters:** At least monthly, but ideally weekly, you should share some valuable newsletter content with your email list to build or maintain the relationship and keep your brand top of mind.

7. **Podcasts:** These are mainly audio interviews with another expert, or you can just record your own thoughts as a diary podcast. They can be on video too. You can record with your smartphone or a small HD digital video camera, or use your laptop to record via Zoom, Skype, Microsoft Teams, Streamyard, or Google Meet. Then you just need to get your show notes together and decide which platforms you'll use to publish it. Apple Podcasts is the biggest network, but Spotify is a close second.

8. **Product images:** If your products have visual appeal and you have great photography or action shots of people using your knives, wineglasses, shoes, artwork, candles, or whatever, share those images on social media to attract customers.

9. **Custom graphics:** Visual images must accompany your blog content when it is shared on social media. Change the images when blogs are shared to keep the content fresh to the audience. Use graphic apps like Canva to customize titles on your artwork.

10. **Roundup posts:** A roundup post is one in which a blogger reaches out to experts, asks one question to each, and then compiles the answers into a single post. This is a great way to get comments, likes, and social shares, and to increase your audience. People love to share their advice.

11. **List posts:** Major magazines are famous for developing lists—for example, "Thirty Top Small Business Podcasts." It doesn't matter what field you're in; a list is a painless way to deliver high-value information to your audience.

12. **Book reviews:** Even people who enjoy reading don't always have time to keep up with new book releases. You can share your perspective on a book with your audience as content on your website.

13. **Case studies:** Write up a case study to share how you helped a client solve a problem. Always highlight the results the clients achieve with your assistance.

14. **Launch a challenge:** If you want to engage your online audience, launch a 3- or 5-Day challenge to get them to take small actions. If you talk about fitness, create a "weight loss challenge." If your content is about selling, set a "week's top sales challenge." It doesn't matter what audience or topic: Challenge them to do something and offer encouragement and additional resources for participation.

15. **Voice search content:** Voice search is an emerging marketing channel. Position your local business to be found by voice assistant devices such as Apple's Siri, Amazon's Alexa, and Google Home.

16. **Alexa flash briefing:** A free content option is a flash briefing. These are short audio clips (ten minutes or less) that are broadcast daily or weekly over an Amazon device. You don't have to have one of these devices to create or listen to an Alexa flash briefing; you can use the Alexa app.

17. **Quiz marketing:** Have you ever seen a quiz pop up when you are on a social media site? Silly, but direct quizzes are actually a powerful content marketing tool to generate qualified leads. Quizzes can convert passive social media followers into leads and eventually paying customers.

18. **Chatbots:** Develop an FAQ, then set up a chatbot on Facebook Messenger to address these customer inquiries. You can set up what's called a chat sequence, which emulates a conversation with a real person. To help the customer reply quickly, you can also use answer prompts, so your customer doesn't have to type.

19. **Chalk:** This app bills itself as the "all-in-one, secure voice headquarters for your community." Essentially, Chalk gives you the ability to have a talk show on your phone anytime you want. You can bring people into your "voice room" to discuss topics, and share pictures too.

20. **Clubhouse:** Clubhouse is a live audio networking platform. You can host your own Clubhouse event any time of the day or night, or schedule and host voice events. Participants can join you on "the stage" to speak, or they can remain in the "audience" to listen.

EMERSON'S essentials

YouTube is the second-most popular search engine online, and how-to videos are the top item searched for in video content. Developing a series of short videos is a great strategy to brand your business. It's a good idea to keep your videos to two minutes or less.

Content marketing doesn't have to be complicated. You're already a subject matter expert. Just remember to have a purpose for every piece of content you create. If you don't have time to write, hire help, especially for editing and social media promotion. Content marketing is a long-tail strategy for a small business, and if you are willing to put the time and effort in, it can really pay off.

When it comes to getting started building your social media footprint, I suggest building a complete profile on LinkedIn first. This is the first place a potential customer will look for information about you. Then, develop a listening strategy to figure out where your best target customer hangs out online, and join that site. Spend some time to learn the best hashtags and keywords for your target customer. Start investing your time with just one social media site first, in order to build a following. Once you feel that you have a dominant brand presence, move on to another site. Do not kill yourself trying to do multiple social media sites every day.

If you are going to leverage social media, you must understand what you can measure about it.

The Triple ROI of Social Media

1. Return on Investment
2. Return on Influence
3. Return on Identity

EMERSON'S essentials

Make a list of the topics you want to cover in your first fifty pieces of content, and start developing them at least two months before launching your website. If you get started ahead of time you'll have content that will keep you going for a while. You just don't want content development to be stressful.

All social media accounts are free, but you must invest your time, which is extremely valuable. Some social media sites offer a paid version, but I have only paid for LinkedIn. If you are successful with social media, you can leverage and monetize your influence. Ultimately you are building your brand identity, which is key because you can hurt your brand as much as you can enhance it. This is why you must be strategic with how you use social media.

Before you start using social media you should have a goal. Are you trying to:

- Build a brand?
- Attract followers, friends, or likes?
- Develop a customer service program?
- Test your pricing or messaging in the market?
- Develop a global customer base?
- Position yourself as a thought leader?
- Drive web traffic?
- Make sales?
- Some combination of these?

It doesn't matter what your goals are, but you need to define them so that you can stay focused with your social media activities.

The HELP Mantra

When you first get started with social media, you should use what I call the HELP mantra. The HELP acronym stands for:

- **Help others first.** Social media is about "Give to get." Any content you share online should be helpful, and you should seek first to add value to the conversation.
- **Engage with people.** Be social and get to know people online. Don't just share links all day. You can't build a relationship if all you do is one-way communication; people want to get to know you.
- **Listen first.** Don't assume you know the culture of the different social media sites. Facebook people may not want to be communicated with in the same way Twitter people would like. Make sure you are communicating in a way that's socially acceptable on the site you're using.
- **Promote yourself with care.** Be sweet, and share other people's content generously. Use the 6-4-1-1 rule of social media. For every six posts you share on your social media channels, four posts should entertain or educate, one post should be a soft sell, and one post should be a hard sell.

Using social media to promote your small business must be an essential part of any new business marketing strategy. But you must be strategic with your time online, as social media can be a huge time suck. (It's easy to lose an hour watching bad dancing on TikTok.) Using social media is a long-term marketing strategy. It will not start raining money in your business the minute you start sharing pictures on Instagram, but if you put the time in, you will eventually see results.

Before getting started, make sure that your website is ready to engage visitors and capture email addresses. You should have at least three offers to entice prospects to join your email list. Your offers could be a free quote, a product sample, a newsletter, or a checklist. You can always provide an ebook highlighting your customers' biggest pain points. For example, if you are starting a business as a real estate agent, you could offer an ebook on *Ten Things You Need to Know Before Buying Your Next House.*

The Six Cs

Follow these six Cs of social media marketing for small businesses to get the most out of your efforts:

1. **Connect:** Use social media to connect with contacts. Forget about collecting paper business cards; you want to connect with new contacts on LinkedIn first. Maintain your profiles on LinkedIn, Facebook, Twitter, YouTube, Pinterest, and Instagram and make sure your profile directs people to how they can do business with you. Avoid personal characterizations like "swim_dad" or "Steelers_fan." Stuff your profiles with keywords, and then dominate with engaging content.

2. **Communicate:** Don't just see how many people you can connect with on social accounts such as LinkedIn, Instagram, Twitter, or Facebook; reach out and communicate with your contacts. If it makes sense, ask to schedule a call or meet in person.

3. **Compelling Content:** If you generate valuable content, the world will beat a path to your door. Decide first whether you will write blogs, record videos or podcasts, or post photos to build your social media brand. Set aside time at least once a week to generate content.

4. **Consistency:** Spend six to twelve months on your number one social media platform sharing other people's content to build

relationships. When you start generating content, keep in mind that you must keep it up or you could damage your brand. Relentless consistency is what it takes to achieve social media success.

5. **Community:** Position yourself as a member of the online community. Use social media daily and engage with people. Thank people who share your content to build rapport. It takes time to build lasting relationships on social media. It can take seven to twenty-one interactions before you have a solid connection online.

6. **Commerce:** Do not try to sell too quickly; you can damage a relationship if a prospect feels like you are not genuine or authentic. If you do your job, your target customers will flock to buy from you. Obviously, you want to sell things, but don't let that be your only agenda for participating in the conversation.

Email Marketing

Email marketing is the fourth leg on your online marketing stool (see Chapter 11). Building an email list is key to the long-term survival of your business; the most valuable asset to any business is its customer list or email list. You can use unique content to nurture your relationships with your potential and existing customers. Email marketing is a cost-effective tool not only to gain new customers but also to retain current ones. The best way to build an email list is to provide a free incentive inviting visitors to subscribe when they land on your website, blog, or one of your social media platforms. These offers can include a direct appeal to sign up for your mailing list, but most people will need a bribe. You can offer discounts, product samples, special reports, guidebooks, checklists, book chapters, video series, podcasts, ebooks, webinars, your newsletter, trial access to your private online community, or a free coaching session.

EMERSON'S experience

To build my email list on my website, https://succeedasyourownboss.com, I offer many free resources, including the ebook *How to Recession Proof Your Small Business*, and I typically create a new ebook offer every six months to attract people to sign up for my email list. I also offer a video series: 7 Tips to Attract Your Ideal Customer. You can register for my weekly *SmallBizLady Buzz* newsletter. I also have dedicated landing pages for all of my online courses, and we use pop-up graphics to promote the courses on specific pieces of content.

One chapter is not enough to cover all there is to know about social media and email marketing, but I have developed three online courses to help you really grasp this information. The first one focuses on building online sales businesses specifically: How to Sell and Market Online. The other two can benefit any business owner: Social Media Selling and The Ultimate Guide to Email Marketing. You can find more information at www.smallbizladyuniversity.com.

Managing Your List

Many business owners use marketing automation software to automate their email marketing efforts. Many of these software options provide easy-to-use online tools and helpful templates for developing email marketing campaigns. My favorite tool is Mixmax; it works with Gmail and all Google Workspace tools. It provides tracking data that tell you how many emails were opened and by whom, which links were clicked on the most, what is the best time of day to send email, whether anyone forwarded the message, and whether anyone opted out of your list. This data is helpful to measure the effectiveness of your email marketing campaigns.

Other popular email marketing services include:

- AWeber
- Constant Contact
- ActiveCampaign

These services have an autoresponder feature designed to send a series of messages to people who sign up for your list. The *Harvard Business Review* says most people only buy after the seventh contact from you. I suggest you set up an email sequence with at least ten messages to be sent over thirty to ninety days.

EMERSON'S essentials

You should never give away something that is not of high value. Giving away products and information is the beginning of a relationship with a potential customer. Do not anger a potential customer by giving away junk. Also, your newsletter may include a special promotion with a call to action, but it had better include information of interest to your readers, or potential customers will unsubscribe quick.

All email marketing services charge a monthly fee, which is based on either the number of people on your list or the number of emails sent each month.

EMERSON'S essentials

Permission is perishable. Once someone gives you his or her email address, a clock starts ticking. You must keep your list engaged and try to convert within ninety days, otherwise you must purge them from your email list if you see that they haven't engaged with your content in 90–180 days.

Things to Keep in Mind

Don't share anything on social media you wouldn't want your grandmother to read. The Internet has a long memory. That said, one negative tweet is not a media crisis; it's just one unhappy customer. Reread your content out loud and listen to your videos carefully before posting anything. Use keywords in your blog titles. Your content title is the most important thing that search engines look at to determine whether your post should be pulled out of the thousands of possible pages and selected as a search result. Use the same keywords somewhere in your text as well.

It doesn't matter if you're an experienced business owner or a novice blogger—everyone reaches a point when they get stuck for content ideas. Focus on solving a problem for your core audience, and you'll always have material for great evergreen content.

If you are posting a video know that your title and description are key to getting it found in YouTube searches. Repurpose your content in newsletters, how-to videos, ebooks, podcasts, and through article marketing sites. Be sure to change at least 20 percent of the content before reposting it, as search engines penalize duplicate content.

EMERSON'S action steps

1. Determine your content strategy (e.g., video, writing, pictures, podcasts).
2. Start developing topics you want to develop to build an archive of great content in advance.
3. Use keywords and hashtags to find out where your target customer spends time online.
4. Spend sixty to ninety minutes a day on social media marketing efforts.
5. Pick five bloggers or media sites you trust to share content from daily.
6. Keep your list engaged. Communicate with subscribers at least monthly.
7. Set aside one day a week to develop new content.
8. Check out online courses How to Sell and Market Online, Social Media Selling, and The Ultimate Guide to Email Marketing at www.smallbizladyuniversity.com.

CHAPTER 13

How to Develop
a Sales Process

One of the biggest challenges many small business owners have is generating consistent sales leads. In any business, you need to have a sales pipeline. I define that as your lead generation and sales funnel process. A sales funnel is the stages that you take prospective customers through during your sales process, known as a customer journey. Once a lead comes into your funnel you leverage email marketing to nurture a relationship and build trust. Then you pitch your offer and stay in front of that potential customer strong for ninety days.

After the sale you continue to nurture the relationship to earn repeat business and engage them as an advocate for your brand. If you start your business without a sales funnel process, you will waste precious time and resources.

From the beginning you want to get organized so that your business will not suffer from the curable condition known as feast or famine sales. This happens when you do a little marketing and land a contract, and then you start working on the contract. Then, thirty days before the contract ends, you look up and realize that you don't have another opportunity in your pipeline, so you panic and start frantically doing marketing again. If you don't have formal sales training, it can easily happen. In this chapter, we'll discuss business-to-business (B2B) sales strategy and business-to-consumer (B2C) sales processes, which will help you avoid this trap.

Lead Generation

How are leads generated? Among other things, through online searches, social media, TV and radio ads, billboards, and magazines. Someone walks into a store, picks up a flyer, clips coupons, or receives direct mail advertising with a discount offer. People experience in-person networking, warm referrals, SMS/text messaging, webinars, social media, email marketing, YouTube video roll-ins, voice device ads, and online ads. Potential customers are bombarded with things to buy, so much so that people pay to not be exposed to advertising. So what is a hungry new business owner to do to find customers? Be strategic, specific, creative, relevant, and timely with your sales efforts.

As a new business, you have limited time and resources, so you should concentrate on the more low-cost sales efforts. In-person leads and warm introductions will be key, and they are handled person-to-person or with a phone call or email. Most of your other sales efforts will be generated online. A potential customer comes to your business website through one of your marketing channels, including your blog, podcast, social media, email, or online ads. That potential customer clicks on your call to action (CTA), which could be an image, link, button, or message that drives an action taking them to the next step in your sales process. Typically, that image or link moves them to a landing page on your website. This page is designed to capture contact information in exchange for an irresistible free offer. (This is discussed in Chapter 12: How to Become a Social Media Activist.) Often landing pages are an offer to make a direct purchase too. Once the form is completed on the landing page, the potential customer should immediately receive a thank-you page that confirms that they have agreed to download your content, or made a purchase and joined your email list. The best thank-you pages provide links to even more information about your brand, such as your latest podcast, video, blog post, or newsletter to help them get to know you. Your freebie offer should arrive in a second email immediately. Then your sales funnel or email sequence should continue over the next ninety days at least to get them to become your customer.

In order to design a sales process let's look at the technology needed to support your sales efforts.

Sales goals are hard to achieve without the right technology and strategy in your sales process. Sales enablement tools offer advancements and conveniences to allow business owners to track sales performance. Here are the top five technology areas to consider to enhance and streamline your sales:

Email

Email is still the most used tool for sales and marketing. Email marketing helps with customer acquisition and retention. If you plan to use email marketing, it would be wise to track the performance of your campaigns. Almost every marketer uses email marketing applications to track open rates and click-throughs. Two of the most popular apps for sales emails are VidReach and Mixmax. VidReach allows you to put a personalized video appeal directly into an email pitch. Mixmax is a marketing automation app that works with Gmail and Google Workspace and integrates with CRM systems such as Pipedrive and Salesforce. It offers email templates and sequences, allows you to set follow-up appointments in one click, and schedules automated emails and follow-ups. There are also apps that will allow you to create interactivity in your emails. You can add polls to learn information from your target customer and calls to action within your emails to drive buyer behavior. These apps provide analytics on the best time to send emails, and will remind you if you haven't followed up within three days to an email someone sent you.

Selling on LinkedIn

There's no better tool online for B2B sales than LinkedIn Sales Navigator. LinkedIn charges $64.99–$103.33 per month for this service depending on the plan. This tool provides courses, consultants, and software to engage prospects, but you could also find a video on YouTube to learn some of these techniques.

Here's a basic step-by-step process for using LinkedIn Sales Navigator:

1. Use the Advanced Search tool to find prospects by industry, professional title, geographic location, and other keywords.
2. Add the leads to your target list.
3. Send an introductory email through LinkedIn to see if they are potential leads.

Write a general email template that you'll use for every contact you research on LinkedIn, but be sure to personalize each one. This is a cold call; you don't have a relationship with this person, so you need to find a specific point of connection. Here are some rules of thumb when it comes to writing emails for prospects on LinkedIn:

Keep It Short

Time is money, so hit them with a question at the beginning of your appeal. The question might focus on a pain point (e.g., "Could you use more sales leads?"). Use only one call to action, and don't use links; they are forbidden in LinkedIn emails.

Focus On Your Subject Line

Your subject line needs to be relevant and useful. For example, one of the most effective email titles is "Quick question."

Personalization Is Everything

Resist the urge to automate your LinkedIn sales activities. Most people who use LinkedIn are bombarded by people trying to sell them services. Personalize your appeal beyond using the person's name or company name. Say something specific about their content or business that drew you to them. You could even send a brief audio recording. The more personal the appeal, the more likely it is that you'll get a response. It takes extra effort, but it's worth it for a six- or seven-figure contract, right?

Communication Tools

Effective communication is the best and only way to sell. You use social media, content, and ads to communicate with prospects and get them to click through to landing pages. However, a communication gap within your internal staff can slow down the sales process. Leverage communication tools such as Slack in order to help your team stay connected so when an order is taken accounting and shipping know. You need a central place where everyone can access the latest product information, logos, collateral materials, or slide decks to use for email pitches or follow-up. You can also leverage Zoom or Google Meet to pitch clients or hold a team meeting.

Competition Tracking

You'll always want to keep an eye on the competition. Check their websites regularly and use Google Alerts to track their brand name and products. Invest your money in competitive analysis too. You can track rivals by utilizing a competition analysis dashboard. If you want to track a competitor's strategic keyword and online ad spend, try apps like SpyFu or iSpionage. Try Sprout Social to figure out a competitor's messaging and see how often they're publishing social content. And use BuzzSumo to look at your top-performing social content and see what is working for your top competitors as well.

Automation

In today's technology-driven world, sales automation software can drive new prospects into your pipeline, screen qualified leads, and enhance your sales funnels. Automation can be used for customer support and client onboarding, internal project management, inventory tracking, and sales enablement. The typical starter sales automation tool is a customer relationship management (CRM) system that allows you to track all communications from phone, email, and social media with prospects and existing customers. It's a good way to keep track of the sales activities once you hire a sales rep too. Good CRM tools for start-ups include Zoho CRM, Pipedrive, and Nimble. Technology not only empowers your sales; it also streamlines your sales process.

Planning a Strategy

Now it's time to start planning your sales strategy. First, take the time to think about how you add value to your customers. What do your customers want to buy, and why should they buy it from you? Put yourself in your customer's shoes. What would convince you to buy from your company? Next, make a list of benefits your customers receive when they choose your company.

EMERSON'S experience

Your sales cycle could be long. It took me four years to close a contract with a major retailer once. I literally had to wait for a woman who was blocking my contract to leave the company, but I never gave up, and I always stayed in touch with other people at the company, so when she did leave I was positioned to get an opportunity.

Find out about what your customers want by listening to them and then help them get what they want. Working on service contracts requires a great deal of time building personal relationships, networking, brainstorming, and providing free consulting before the contract (this can be dangerous since you don't want to get used with no contract in sight), but mostly it will work out. Then you want to thank your main contact for the opportunity and provide great service after the sale. If you put in the legwork up front, you are set. At that point, your price will no longer be an issue, because your contact will likely tell you their budget.

Ask your target customers these key questions:

- Why are they searching for a product or solution?
- Where are they in their search process?
    - Do they have a budget?
    - Have they created a request for proposal (RFP)?
- How many vendors are competing?
- How will the decision process be handled?

- What is their timeline for completion?
- How does purchasing from you factor into their business goals?
  - Do you help generate revenue?
  - Do you decrease costs?
  - Are you helping them fill a need or desire to work with a local business or other specific group (e.g., minority, women, disabled veterans, LGBT).

How to Develop a Sales Process for B2B Sales

If you start running your business without a sales process, you might develop bad habits. Here are eleven strategies you can use as you develop a B2B sales process:

1. Develop a Target List

Start your sales process by identifying potential customers. Develop a customer target list of fifty to a hundred companies or agencies you want to target. Then, reach out to your connections and see who knows someone at the companies you want to target. LinkedIn is great for this kind of research. Do your homework on these companies; I suggest picking three to five a week to study. If they are publicly traded, pull the 10K report, and if Wall Street is talking about the firm, subscribe to Owler to track the company. Put a Google Alert on the company's name to track media mentions and any trigger events. Follow your targets across social media to learn as much as you can about your potential customers.

2. Build a Detailed Profile of Your Targets

The leading social media network for B2B companies is LinkedIn. It's a hub for professionals in any industry and ideal for tracking down information to build a business relationship online. Consider tools like

Nimble or Qualtrics to find out who the decision-makers are and their full contact information. Once you have contact information for the decision-maker, friend-raise first. Try to build a relationship the best you can; ask about pain points before you mention anything about pitching for business. Focus on what you can offer the business first.

3. Only Sell to Your Niche Customer

Every customer is not necessarily your customer. Go after your niche hard. Specialists charge more and are in higher demand. When you are fishing for customers, it's best to offer them the bait that they love to eat! Avoid competing on price, if you can. It's best to try to sweeten the deal with an add-on not specified in the scope of work. It takes more effort, and you'll be lowering your profit margin, but if you're willing to invest in your client, and do a great job, you could have a client for life.

4. Develop Consistent Sales Habits

Marketing is something that you must do two hours a day. Or, dedicate two days a week to only marketing to build up your sales muscles. Once you have a target list, determine how you will engage your potential customers. You can make phone calls, send emails, create videos, conduct podcast interviews, share articles, mail books, or send handwritten notes. Contact customers every other month or at least quarterly to stay in regular contact. Start a birthday list or pick another holiday where you reach out to them all. Valentine's Day is a good day to contact customers to share some love.

5. Try Webinars

Webinars are a great lead magnet, and they give you an email list of hot leads to follow up on. You should host webinars that provide value on a topic that hits a major pain point for potential buyers. You want to attract customers who are struggling with an issue. Provide some solutions, but never give away everything. You always want to close with an offer with a specific deadline. Design your webinar to revolve around the value you're providing, leading up to a well-placed, compelling call to action to close sales.

6. Keep Your Name Out There

Attend networking activities, industry conferences, trade shows, procurement fairs, Women's Business Enterprise National Council (WBENC) and National Minority Supplier Development Council (NMSDC) conferences, and pre-bid meetings. Look for speaking opportunities. Participate in virtual summits, panels, TED Talks, local business events, and conferences. You want people to know that you are in business full time and ready for an opportunity.

7. Be Relentless, but Don't Be a Pest

To make a sale you must stay in front of your customers. Start with a personal follow-up then use email or direct mail to familiarize potential customers with your company and how you can help. Use email platforms or direct mail firms such as Vistaprint or Mail Shark to keep in touch with a color postcard mailer. No matter what you send, it always must be followed up with a phone call. B2B selling is not mass marketing; you can make the calls. Sales magic can happen over the phone.

8. Prepare for the Sales Meeting

Consider your first meeting as a fact-finding mission where you are asking questions, listening for ways to solve their problems. It's best to be more interested than interesting. Find out who will be at the meeting. Look them up on LinkedIn and study their background for points of connection. Don't go there to pitch, but be ready to pitch if someone asks for more information. Remember, the meeting is not about your pitch. Ask how they do business, how they award contracts, and what they like and dislike from a supplier. After the meeting, always send a handwritten thank-you note. It's about learning the needs of your customers and seeing who has the juice to sign a deal.

9. Develop a Winning Proposal

After you receive the request for a proposal, you must create a winning proposal. If possible, request a meeting to present it. Your proposal should entice customers to buy from your company. Use visuals and photographs of case studies of your prior work. Explain how you have solved problems for your customers. Offer to allow them to talk to one of your other customers. Convince them why they should buy only from you. Make sure your pitch overcomes their fears and concerns and price objections, and tell them how you will reduce their risk. Ask for the business, and price the job to make a profit. Competing on price is dangerous; focus on the value you will provide.

10. Follow Up Aggressively

Your fortune is in your follow-up. Follow up within forty-eight hours after your submission to show you are interested in working with them. If the customer doesn't return your calls, leave messages with additional ideas about how your company can perform better or save him or her time or money. Don't give up. And, if you are not successful, ask for a feedback meeting to learn what (other than price) you might be able to fix for the next time.

11. Use Project Management Software to Track Milestones

Have regular meetings with the client and your core team. Always follow up meetings with an email with the next steps, timelines, and deliverables. Be sure to note any deadline corrections or scope changes. After the project ends, send a thank-you note and a token gift of flowers, a fruit basket, a gift card to their favorite restaurant, or a wine basket, if their company policies permit it.

B2C Selling

Now let's look at B2C, or direct-to-consumer selling. According to a study from the Interactive Advertising Bureau on "The Rise of the 21st Century Brand Economy," the future of retail growth will come from direct-to-consumer relationships. Selling to consumers is an art form that requires many different tools to get the job done. There are many things that can drive sales, including seasonality, consumer demand, promotional merchandising, and pricing and sales. Identifying leads is only the first step. Convincing them to actually buy your product requires a forward-thinking sales plan.

Tell an Honest Story about Your Product

The brand story is not really about the product; it's why people buy. Every business has a story to tell, whether it's how they were founded or why they launched the business. Is your business a hobby that turned into a lucrative business? Or is your story more like that of MamaSuds? The owner of that business developed a line of nontoxic cleaning products made with pure essential oils after her child came down with an illness and no commercial soap would work for him. Our brains process the human emotions behind the story, and that creates the connection, which drives people to become brand ambassadors.

In-Person Shopping Must Run Alongside the Online Selling Experience

Online selling and brick-and-mortar retail must go together because the competitive landscape has shifted. People want options. Can I come to the store, try on, and buy with tap and pay? Can I order the product and have it shipped free? Can I order online and come pick it up today? What about hassle-free returns? As business owners, we must give people what they want.

Sell a Product, Not an Experience

Customer experience (CX) is driving so much about consumer sales. From the social images to the packaging to the unboxing experience, brands that pay attention to small details are winning.

Bundle and Win

In retail stores people want to find what they need quickly. Try setting up a special area for new products. Make good use of window displays and outdoor signage. Use other creative display methods to direct their attention to popular items. Always have seasonal tie ins and holiday displays. Use point-of-purchase displays and product bundles to cross-sell related items too.

Leverage Presale Orders

Offer gift cards or discounts for presale orders (e.g., at a salon offer three facials for $125). Everyone loves a deal and you need the cash flow, so see what you can offer that your client will love so much that they are willing to prepay. Make sure the prepayment has an expiration date; six months is a fair amount of time.

Develop Customer Personas

Understanding who your customers are and why they buy is key to engaging them in meaningful conversations. You want to be positioned to recommend products and services most relevant to their needs. When you are a small business owner doing your own sales and online engagement, it is important to develop a marketing message that will resonate with your target customers. Using customer personas will inform your selling process and drive greater customer satisfaction, which can build customer loyalty and increase sales.

Customer personas are fictional customer personalities that you create, based on your niche customer. It's like a profile that represents real customers and highlights who they are and where they live, as well as their lifestyle, pain points, habits, and goals that inform their buying decisions. You can have several different customer personas depending on the type of business you have.

Everyone, Meet Sharon

Imagine that you own a medical spa in Philadelphia. "Sharon" could be a customer persona you might develop for your business: Sharon is forty-two and married with two college-age children. She works in the city as a paralegal for a boutique law firm. She works long hours, often six days a week. She lives in the suburbs with her husband. Sharon is into skin care and maintaining her youthful beauty. She had bad acne as a teen. She works out at home two or three days a week. She makes a good salary and has some disposable income, and she believes that investing in beauty care and professional treatments is worth it. She is known for always dressing nicely, and her makeup is always perfect.

Priorities
- Getting ahead at work
- Meeting fitness goals
- Enhancing beauty through anti-aging treatments
- Having energy to sustain long hours
- Having time to spend with her family

Pain Points
- Workaholic
- Little time for self-care
- Concerned about anti-aging facial treatments
- High cost of plastic surgery
- Poor value from online facial product options

Preferred Channels

- Facebook
- Email
- Text messaging
- Google search

Sharon is an example of a persona—an imaginary customer. Once you have your personas, give each persona a name, include a photo, and describe their attributes. You can create PowerPoint slides describing the personas in order to train your team and any salespeople you may bring on later. You can even put up posters of your personas around the office as a reminder for everyone to stay customer-focused.

EMERSON'S essentials

You create customer personas from real interview data collected from prospects. Use social media to solicit interviews for potential customers. It always helps to persuade people to participate if you offer a gift card, product sample, ebook, or checklist. Remember to keep any survey short: no more than five to seven questions.

Once you know who your potential customers are, what they care about, and where they spend time online, you'll know how to craft messages that appeal to them. Without a reliable sales process to follow, your sales will underperform. If you want to eliminate feast or famine in your business, the only route to success is to develop a sales process with the right knowledge, tools, and strategies.

EMERSON'S action steps

1. Develop consistent sales habits.
2. If you sell B2B, learn how to use LinkedIn Sales Navigator.
3. Get your sales technology in place, especially CRM and competition tracking.
4. Get clear about your brand story.
5. Develop customer personas.

CHAPTER 14

·SELLING ONLINE

Nearly every business can benefit from selling online. While most physical products can and should be sold online, you can also sell services online. For example, if you own a salon, you could allow clients to book their appointments—and even prepay for those services—online. Consultants can sell consulting packages, construction companies can use tools to process installment payments online, and all kinds of businesses can benefit from selling gift certificates. There are many tools to set up e-commerce on your website. Some popular options include:

- WooCommerce (WordPress plugin)
- Shopify (excellent for physical products)
- BigCommerce
- ThriveCart
- Ontraport

191

- PayPal
- Square
- Stripe

You will need to research features with each e-commerce service to find the one that best matches your needs. For example, not all e-commerce solutions are built to handle digital product sales. Services like Square are useful for processing sales in person, using a smartphone, and you can also send digital invoices. PayPal is a good starter option if you plan to have only a handful of products for sale on your site. Make sure to do your homework.

If you are ready to enter the online market, there are two things you need to decide: whether you will sell on your own website or on a marketplace site, and how much monthly budget you will have to spend on online ads. To build your own business website requires significant investment. You'll need to build a brand and drive traffic to your website by leveraging strategic content, SEO, landing pages, social media, and paid ads. The key benefits from building your own site are you have the opportunity to build a direct relationship with your customers, conduct marketing campaigns, and build brand customer loyalty. You can also sell on a marketplace site such as Amazon, eBay, Walmart, or Etsy. The advantages of joining a marketplace are they have a huge amount of traffic, visitors are ready to buy, and you can create a seller account and start selling within hours. The downsides are there's a ton of competition among sellers, there's no personalization, you don't own your customer list, and you must pay a percentage of every sale to the marketplace.

Before Paying for Online Ads

One of the first places you'll need to invest once your site is built is online ads. Whether you choose to go with pay-per-click (PPC) or social media ads, there are several things you need to think about for online advertising:

Determine Your Budget

Setting an ad spend budget in advance puts you in better control of the advertising process and helps you determine how much you will spend and at which stage. You should have enough budget to invest in a marketing campaign for at least six months.

Research

Carry out research before you launch ad campaigns. This includes granular details about the market you are targeting, developing a keyword strategy, and evaluating competitors' positions in the market.

Keywords Research for PPC Ads

If you fail to create a list of quality keyword phrases, your ads may not perform well. Use Google's free Keyword Planner tool to create a list of effective keywords that you'll be using in your ads.

Audience Research for Social Media Ads

Creating ads without defining the target audience is a recipe for disaster. That's why your ads need to be created for a specific audience for better conversions. Social platforms like Facebook and Instagram allow businesses to get granular in ad targeting with the help of detailed audience research.

Create a High-Converting Landing Page

If your ad is successful and the prospect clicks a link to come to your sales page, also known as a landing page, you want to make sure it's designed to convert visitors into buyers. A high-converting landing page has fast load speed and unique and engaging content supported by great visuals.

Capture Visitor Contact Info

Not every visitor will purchase on the first visit. When new prospects land on your website or landing page, you want to be able to capture their information so that you can connect with them and grow sales. Use lead generation forms to capture contact information. You will use that information to launch your sales funnel and to send nurture emails and promotional offers to convert interested visitors into customers in the future. (More on sales funnels in Chapter 13: How to Develop a Sales Process.)

Decide How You Will Measure Success

Decide what you want to achieve with your campaigns, how you want to reach your sales goals, and over what period of time. This should guide you when setting performance metrics, and will be helpful when evaluating performance so you can make an informed budget decision on whether to keep investing.

Selling on Amazon

Amazon is the biggest online e-commerce site in the US, generating more online sales than any other platform. There are twelve million items available on Amazon, and according to *Inc.* there are one million small businesses currently selling there. In fact, according to Small Business Trends, 60 percent of small businesses in the US drive more than half of their online sales on e-commerce sites like Amazon and eBay. So, it comes as no surprise that 68 percent of small business owners say Amazon has positively impacted their online sales.

To be able to list yourself as an Amazon seller and start selling on this platform, follow these steps:

Create a Seller Account

If you don't have a personal or seller account on Amazon, you need to create one. Before you sign up, keep the following information ready, as you'll need it in the process:

- Your business email address or your Amazon customer account
- A chargeable credit card
- Government ID proof for the verification process
- Tax information
- Contact number
- A bank account where Amazon can submit payments

Select a Plan

Amazon offers two types of plans: individual and professional. If you choose the individual plan, you'll pay $0.99 for every item sold. The professional plan costs a flat monthly fee of $39.99 irrespective of how many products you sell. There are additional charges like the variable referral fee that Amazon deducts against each transaction. Go to https://sellercentral .amazon.com/ to select a plan.

Create a Selling Strategy

One of the top sales strategies is to start off with a small inventory and scale up based on which items are most successful. Start with a few items that your research has shown will likely do well, build up your reputation, and test out more items gradually.

Product Listing

Once your seller account is set up, start with creating your first product listing. An Amazon product listing is made up of three different parts: the title, the key features, and the product description. Next, you'll need to upload high-resolution images. You will also need to update shipping information, fill in other mandatory details, and then submit your product. You will see the listing activated within a few minutes.

How to Become Amazon's Choice

Products marked as "Amazon's Choice" are those that have generated enormous sales, are fairly priced, and have met customer satisfaction. If you hover the mouse near the Amazon's Choice button it says: "Amazon's Choice recommends highly rated and well-priced products." Products with this tag are likely to generate more sales, so if you want your products to have this tag, ensure that your products:

- Are eligible for Amazon Prime shipping
- Are always in stock
- Have a great sales track record
- Receive high customer ratings

How to Get Your Products Available for Prime Shipping

Prime shipping is one of the most preferred shipping choices for customers because it's free, fast, and reliable. Prime-eligible products receive more visibility, are higher ranking, and get more sales. Here are the ways to make your product eligible for Prime shipping:

Sellers must have fulfilled a minimum of thirty Premium Shipping (Same-Day Delivery and/or Two-Day Shipping) orders in the previous thirty calendar days.

To qualify for Prime shipping you must provide or have:

- A tracking ID for 94 percent or more orders.
- An on-time delivery rate of 96 percent or higher.
- A cancellation rate of under 1 percent.

Fulfillment by Amazon

Fulfillment by Amazon (FBA) is a comprehensive, pay-as-you-go service provided by Amazon to sellers. How it works: You send your items to Amazon by following their standard guidelines, and after that, Amazon takes care of warehousing, packing, shipping and handling, returns, and customer service. If you have limited resources and time to handle the back-end delivery, FBA is ideal for you.

Vendor Central

Unlike selling directly to shoppers, sellers at Vendor Central sell to Amazon and act as wholesale suppliers. However, this is an invitation-only feature, and you need to be contacted by Amazon to become a vendor and participate.

How to Run Amazon Ads for Your Products

Amazon ads work similarly to Google search ads (discussed later in this chapter). As buyers type in relevant keywords or search phrases on the search bar, both organic and paid listings that have the same or similar keywords appear in the results. Small business owners who want to gain quick visibility should try different ad formats. These are pay-per-click (PPC) ads, which means you only pay when someone clicks on your ad.

Ad types on Amazon are:

Sponsored Products

Sponsored product ads are one of the most common ad types. As buyers search for products, Amazon pulls up your sponsored ads and shows them alongside organic listings based on your bidding strategy and places them in various target locations. Eligible sellers include the professional sellers, book vendors, and Kindle Direct Publishing (KDP) authors.

Sponsored Brands

Sponsored brands are PPC banner ads that display your brand logo, custom tag line, and multiple products, typically at the top of Amazon search results. In early 2020, Amazon released a new feature that allows brands to create video ads that will appear in the search results.

Sponsored Display Ads

Sponsored display ads are simple PPC ads that don't need a large budget. Sponsored display advertising offers three targeting options:

- Views Targeting: Works great if you want to remarket your ads to re-engage your audience. Remarket ads target people who previously interacted with your products or brand on Amazon.
- Product Targeting: Ads based on products you specify.
- Interest Targeting: Raise brand awareness by targeting shoppers with specific interests.

Amazon's dominance in e-commerce is undeniable, and it offers a wealth of opportunities for both sellers and buyers. With smart strategies, pricing models, and a customer-centric approach, you can easily achieve great success by selling on Amazon. Along with selling online, you should know how to promote your products online. Now let's discuss the types of online ads and strategies.

Pay-Per-Click Ads

PPC ads are a popular search engine advertising model. Sites like Google, YouTube, Facebook, and Amazon offer PPC advertising. It is a paid marketing method in which you show relevant ads to searchers based on their search queries with the goal of converting them into customers. With PPC ads, while you only pay when someone clicks on that ad, the cost can range from $0.10 to $20.00 per click depending on the competition and demand for the keyword or phrase. There are various PPC ad types, including text-based ads, local ads, and shopping ads; they offer advertisers an array of ways to land in front of their target audience.

With growing competition in organic search results, PPC is becoming increasingly popular among small businesses across many industries. Here are some of the benefits of PPC ads for small businesses:

Measurable ROI

PPC ads make it easy for you to track ad performance and spending. And you can evaluate your return on investment (ROI) with analytics. This helps you to make an informed decision for reaching your business goals and to forecast buyer behavior and sales performance.

Boost Traffic to Your Site

It's no secret that SEO and organic search marketing take time to show results. So, if you want to drive visitors to your site, PPC ads can be a fast and effective way to do so.

Remarket and Bring Back Lost Leads

With remarketing ads, you can target buyers who didn't make a purchase after browsing your site and place ads to entice them back when they go other places online.

How to Use Google Ads

Google Ads enable small businesses to target locally, which is especially useful if you operate in limited local areas or are a retailer. Specific targeting gives you maximum exposure, greater ROI, and helps increase sales revenue.

Google created Smart Campaigns for small businesses; it's easy to use, can be set up quickly, and is used to launch ads to drive traffic to generate leads. There is no minimum ad spend on Google, so small businesses can position ads without having a big budget. You can pay as you go, which makes it easy to have more control on your ad spends.

How Google Ads Work: Keywords, Keywords, Keywords

Keywords, or "search terms," are the heart of all Google Ads. These are the words and phrases your prospective customers would use to search for your services or products online. You want to identify as many keyword phrases as possible for your ad campaigns to ensure you're serving up relevant ads that convert to new revenue.

Google PPC ads are driven by keywords. Online advertisers select relevant target keyword phrases and develop bidding strategies to drive traffic to their site. Advertisers choose between search ads and display ads when setting up ad campaigns on Google.

- Ads on the Display Network let users display visual marketing materials like banners and images on targeted websites.
- PPC campaigns allow advertisers to bid on keywords and win their position on search results pages.

There are several types of Google Ads to choose from to optimize for best performance:

Search Ads

Search ads are the most popular text-based PPC ads that appear on top of and below organic results on the search engine results pages (SERP).

Display Ads

Display advertisements on Google are distributed across websites like YouTube and apps that are part of Google Display Network. Unlike search ads, you can use images and text for your display ads.

Shopping Ads

Google shopping ads are a great way to target bottom-of-the-funnel customers and generate leads and eventually sales. Bottom-of-the-funnel is the last stage in the buyer's journey when a qualified lead makes a purchasing decision. These ads are displayed when buyers search for specific products online.

Local Service Ads

If your business provides a service such as plumbing, snow removal, or pest control, and you're looking for local customers and leads, Google's Local Services Ads are best for your business. With these ads, you can feature your services to online shoppers in your own community on a desktop or mobile device.

Retargeting Ads

Retargeting ads let you target leads who once visited your website or clicked on an ad but didn't make a purchase. Your ads will essentially follow the visitor around the Internet and display ads on websites and apps they visit until they purchase from you or the ad expires.

Great Tools to Build and Measure Ad Campaigns

Google offers a variety of free tools to help small businesses create, promote, and audit ad campaigns. For keyword research, you can head to Google Keyword Planner to find the keyword(s) that you'll want to use for maximum impact in search queries.

The Google Ads Keyword Planner is a free tool that you can use to build strong keyword lists and get started with your ad campaigns. With this tool, you can generate keyword ideas and even calculate bid estimates for specific keywords before building an ad campaign strategy.

For performance measurement, the reporting features in Google Ads allow you to access, analyze, and evaluate the impact of your ads so you can continually optimize them for maximum return.

Google has adopted two different strategies for keyword usage: one for search ads and the other for display ads.

Search Network Campaigns

For running Search Network Campaigns, choose relevant keywords that match your theme. Pay close attention to terms like "exact match," "phrase match," and "broad match" because if you select the wrong match type or wrong keywords, your ads might not appear.

Display Network Campaigns

For choosing keywords for Display Network Campaigns, start by creating separate ad groups targeting products or services you offer, and then select specific keywords that are relevant for each of these ad groups. These are visual-based ads you typically see while reading blogs, watching YouTube, or using an app on a mobile device.

Social Media Advertising

Social media advertising is the process of locating your audience on social media platforms and driving sales through paid campaigns. In some cases, you can actually convert sales directly through some platforms if you have the right product or service offer. The following are some of the most popular social media platforms with billions of active users where you can showcase your products using social ads and increase sales revenue.

Facebook

More than 2.7 billion people are active on Facebook around the globe. Facebook offers a robust advertising platform that allows small businesses a number of targeting criteria for their ads, thus making it easier to land in front of your ideal customer. According to Statista, among brands and businesses that are active on Facebook, 96 percent are B2C brands, and 91 percent are business-to-business (B2B) brands, which means any business could benefit from investing in Facebook ads. This is good news because Facebook could be your answer regardless of whether you're selling products or services. Because Facebook reaches so many users, advertising here can be effective for all kinds of businesses. Here's how to generate leads, and convert them to sales, with Facebook ads:

Exact Audience Targeting

Facebook has a great deal of information about their users. Their ad platform allows you to target specific audiences based on their interests, age range, locations, demographics, income, language, and keywords.

Boost Winning Content

Leveraging content that is already popular on Facebook gives you a better chance of generating sales. Identify your past content that generated more engagement and was widely accepted by your audience. Create your ad around those topics and content.

Use Multi-Product Carousel Ads

With the multi-product carousel ad format, you can use up to ten images or videos, each with a custom link. This gives you the freedom to showcase a wider range of products in a single ad and target more buyers and generate more sales. The carousel ad format is available for Facebook and Instagram.

Custom CTA (Call to Action)

Facebook allows businesses to create custom calls to action in ads, which allows more control over conversion.

Ad Remarketing

Just as with Google, you can also create remarketing ads on Facebook and target your lost leads and convert them to a sale.

EMERSON'S essentials

The secret to selling more with Facebook is to keep your content relevant and specific to your target audience. By getting granular, you can narrow your target audience to increase Facebook ad relevancy, and lower the ad expenses. If your ads aren't meeting your sales objectives, you can use Facebook's ad relevance diagnostics to understand whether adjustments to your creative assets, post-click experience, or audience targeting could improve performance.

Instagram

The photo-sharing platform Instagram has over one billion active users every month, so there's a good reason for you to explore this platform.

The Instagram ad platform is effective for both B2B and B2C industries actively looking to promote brands, generate sales, and create brand awareness. Global users are 52 percent female and 48 percent male. Instagram users are 58 times more likely to engage with businesses and ads than on Facebook. They're also 120 times more likely to engage with brands on Instagram than on Twitter. The Instagram community not only engages with ads; they also remember the brands they've engaged with. Here's how you can get started with Instagram ads:

Set Up an Instagram Business Account

Business profiles give you access to in-depth Insights and Instagram Analytics about your audience, but they also enable you to use the following features:

- Instagram Shopping
- Instagram contact button
- Food delivery and gift card stickers and buttons
- "Get Tickets" button to sell tickets
- Schedule appointments button

Brand Your Instagram Bio

Create a perfectly branded landing page that sends a never-ending stream of traffic from your Instagram bio to your most important content.

Get Visibility with Hashtags

A hashtag is a combination of words, numbers, or emojis preceded by the pound sign, aka the hash (#) symbol (e.g., #womeninbusiness). Hashtags are used to categorize content generally and make it more searchable. They are clickable on Instagram. Anyone who conducts a hashtag search will see a page showing posts tagged with that hashtag on Instagram. If you use a hashtag on your story, it also appears on the hashtag page. People can choose to follow hashtags too. It's a great way to build community online and motivate people to engage with your brand and your ads.

Use Great-Quality Visuals and Minimal Text

If you want your Instagram ads to yield results, use high-quality, original images, descriptive captions or a single text that can be a promo code, or a statement inside the image.

EMERSON'S essentials

When it comes to Instagram ads, your goal should be to show a single picture with a direct link to buy that item. Don't make it complicated for the shopper; get them to the product without unnecessary distractions.

Create Instagram Stories

People love stories. Create eye-catching, immersive ads with images and videos that run on Instagram Stories. Remember that stories last only for twenty-four hours, so try to make the best of it. Convey your message within the image and add a compelling CTA to make it more effective.

Ad Retargeting

Launch Instagram ad campaigns to target those who added your products but abandoned their carts without making a purchase. Remarketing or retargeting is a great way to convert already generated leads to customers.

Facebook Ads Integration

All Instagram ads are integrated with the Facebook ad platform. You get access to the granular audience targeting and customized settings for both.

YouTube

YouTube is a unique advertising platform that unlocks access to various ad categories and gives you the freedom to choose what suits your business and budget. You can select from a range of ad types—skippable to non-skippable video ads, bumper ads to masthead ads, and others. Because YouTube is owned by Google, advertising on the platform provides many of the same reach benefits you'll find with the Google Display Network (GDN) including:

Keyword Targeting

You can create your ad campaign using specific keywords across YouTube and GDN. This makes it easy for your ad to show up when people search for similar content.

Select Ad Format

From skippable to non-skippable, display ads to overlay ads, bumper to sponsored card ads, you have plenty of ad format choices with YouTube.

You should invest time in reading which type of format works best for you. As a beginner you may not have the exact answer, so you can try to experiment with various formats and stick to what generates more sales.

In-Market Buyer Groups

Discover your niche audiences who are actively researching products or services you offer and target them for higher ad conversions. You can even target by gender, age group, and other demographics.

Do Research on Successful Ads

Do some research and find the best-performing ads on YouTube. Study their style, and take note of what you like most about these ads. As you generate keywords for your ad campaign, add any relevant keywords from your research in your ad copy; otherwise your ads will not be visible in search results. Also integrate your campaign with Google Analytics to make it easier for you to monitor audience behavior and understand what works best.

Video Remarketing

Connect with viewers based on their past interaction with your videos and increase sales revenue by converting them into customers.

For more information on how to set up your online ads, check out my course How to Sell and Market online at www.smallbizladyuniversity.com.

EMERSON'S action steps

1. Decide where you will sell online: custom URL or marketplace?
2. Use the Google Keyword Planner to choose keyword phrases.
3. Write irresistible headlines.
4. Keep your ads relevant and targeted, especially on social media.
5. Set a daily budget that allows you to properly test your ads, before you make a major investment.

CHAPTER 15

SETTING UP SHOP

Where do you plan to locate your business? World headquarters for many multimillion dollar businesses started on a kitchen table, on a corner desk in a bedroom, in a basement, or in a garage. Great ideas and ambition can percolate just about anywhere. What is most important is the vision and hard work of the entrepreneur.

Getting Started

Success can change your geography over time from a kitchen table to a boardroom, but what do you need to get started? Here are some rules to consider:

Let Growth Drive Expansion

Keep your overhead as low as possible. Run your business from your house or apartment until it becomes almost impossible to keep up with sales and inventory in the space you have (watch out for zoning regulations, however; they might cause problems).

EMERSON'S experience

Do not use your home address for your business. Rent a mailbox at a UPS Store, which will give you a real street address. You can also rent a P.O. Box from the local post office. When my business started to grow, and I started to get media attention, I got scary letters from strange people and prisoners at my home address. People also dropped by unannounced looking for work. As well, I got—and still get—an incredible amount of small business junk mail. Remember, you need to protect your privacy.

Look for Inexpensive Space

There are coworking spaces popping up in cities everywhere. Another option is to join a business incubator or accelerator. There are also Impact Hub locations across the country for businesses that are social ventures. Regus (https://regus.com) is a for-profit option to rent a conference and office space when you need it. They are located in most major cities, but their options can get pricey.

Get all of the information you can so you can get the right space at the right price. Look for business owners with excess space to sublet or share a few days a week. I have a coaching client who is a therapist. He only sees patients three times a week in the evenings, so he shares space with a dermatologist who stops seeing patients at 4 p.m. each day.

Invest In a Good Computer and Backup

Start with a new laptop with a quality color printer. Be sure to get the three-year crash and burn platinum warranty. You cannot afford to have your computer down for one hour and certainly not for three days. Purchase a thumb drive or invest in a cloud system to back up your files. Dropbox is useful software. Your computer is your "brains in a box"—it can help to write proposals, email customers, track your budget and sales, manage subcontractors, order supplies, look up sales information, create and monitor your task lists, and a ton of other stuff. You can get what you need for $850–$2,000.

Be on the lookout for sales and special deals. Around holiday time, when retailers are trying to clear their inventories, is a great time to buy electronics for your business. Salespeople are often willing to make you a deal so they can get their bonus. Save all receipts; you can write off the purchase against your taxes for the year. Talk to your accountant about how much of an investment you can make in your business. Remember, only spend what's in your financial plan's budget.

Store Your Stuff

You need a home for accounting records, receipts, bills of lading, order forms, invoices, brochures, tax information, incorporation information, and lots of other paperwork. A four-drawer file cabinet, hanging file folders, regular file folders, and a sense of order are just the ticket, especially if the IRS ever audits you. Keep your personal and business information separate to minimize confusion and to simplify your operation. It also makes it easier for you or your bookkeeper to track spending and receipts and determine whether you are actually making money. When you make a bank deposit, write on the deposit receipt whom the check was from and the amount. Make a copy of all checks from clients. Get a fireproof safe to store blank checks, important papers, and any software that you've purchased. When you pay invoices it is a good idea to record on the invoice the date and check number you used to assist your bookkeeper with the financial records.

Buy Secondhand When You Can

Recessions always create opportunities to buy used or refurbished desks, tables, chairs, bookshelves, and other equipment. In many cases, you will save up to 75–80 percent off retail. Two great places to look for this kind of stuff are www.freecycle.org and www.craigslist.org. The Freecycle Network is a cool organization that makes it easy for people to post notices to give away unwanted items for free. Its mission is to build a worldwide gifting movement in order to reduce waste.

Look around for the best quality you can find. There are plenty of secondhand furniture stores. Talk to friends who still work in the corporate world and find out if they know of companies selling used furniture.

EMERSON'S experience

When I first started my business, my brother worked for DuPont. They had a sale of old furniture. We shopped for my first file cabinets there and got some great deals. Just make sure that the drawers work, the legs are securely attached to all chairs, and that it's reasonably clean. Measure your available space to make sure what you're buying fits. The time to buy new will come later when you start to make money.

Plan Communication

How will your customers reach you? A cell phone can be a virtual office, giving access to you any time or any place, but the signal can be weak or disrupted, giving the customer a less-than-professional impression of your business. Make sure you have a landline phone or VoIP service. Get a professional headset.

Create a voice mailbox and make sure the greeting you record is polished and professional. Remember, your phone is the lifeline to sales. You want to be easy to do business with. Look for phone service packages that offer the biggest discounts. Also, be aware of termination fees and contract requirements. If you have a business that is driven by appointment setting you might need live call center support, from a service like Ruby.

Purchase Business Insurance

If you rent office space, secure a business property insurance policy. Even if you work from home you will need a separate policy to protect your business assets. You will also need liability insurance to protect you from a lawsuit should any of your products or services result in someone being injured or in property being damaged. Your vendors will typically require a copy of your liability policy to be included with an RFP form. Some even require to be listed as additionally insured on your policy.

If you have employees you will also need workers' compensation insurance. This will protect you and your employees should anyone be hurt on the job. The cost of this insurance is high, but it varies based on the types of workers you have and the level of risk involved in their job functions. I have found that the cheapest option for workers' compensation is to buy it from your state. Regardless, you must have workers' compensation insurance if you have employees. It's the law.

Leasing As an Option

Consider leasing office equipment instead of buying it. There are several advantages to this strategy, the most important being an improvement in your cash position. A loan to purchase equipment requires at least 25 percent of the loan in cash up front. Other than a refundable security deposit, equipment leases require no money down. Additional benefits include:

- Easier financing than a purchase. Leasing companies typically want a year or less of business credit history before approving a lease of furniture or office equipment. Capital equipment loans require three years of financial history.

- Leasing means you will not be stuck with obsolete equipment. You can do a short-term lease, which swaps out the equipment every one to two years. There's always a faster, cheaper model coming out for copiers, printers, and postage meters. If you lease a copier, make sure you really need it. If you pay the lease fee as well as a per copy fee, it might be cheaper to go to the corner store to make your copies.
- Leasing helps the bottom line in more ways than one. Your accountant may be able to recategorize some assets on your balance sheet. Your firm's debt-to-equity ratio will look much healthier, as will your earnings-to-fixed-assets ratio. Keep in mind that under certain types of agreements, the lease contract will be reported as an asset on your balance sheet and taxes.

When leasing office equipment:

- Shop around for the best financing deal.
- Make sure you can break the lease agreement if you have to. Note the cost of the penalty fee.
- Don't lease for more than two years.
- Look for an option-to-buy clause.
- Negotiate a "modern equipment substitution clause" that lets you trade up for the latest technology.

EMERSON'S action steps

1. Let your business drive your growth; work from home until the business operations require professional office space.

2. Get your first office space on the cheap. Look for a small business incubator, or sublet or share space with another entrepreneur who has a similar business or works opposite hours.

3. Create an internal communications plan (phone, voice mail, Internet, cell phone with email capability).

4. Store your important records and receipts properly so you can find them later when you need them.

5. Buy used when you can. Consider leasing office equipment, but run the numbers to make sure it's a good deal.

6. Get yourself a business address other than your home.

7. Get yourself a good computer with a three-year crash and burn warranty and a backup system. Don't go cheap! This is the brain of your business.

8. Look into all the business insurance that you may need: property, liability, health, and workers' compensation.

CHAPTER 16

BUILD YOUR TEAM

When you can no longer survive as an "army of one," it is time to bring reinforcements...employees. Hiring and working with employees will be an adjustment, but it's one you will thank yourself for later, particularly if you choose well. Five months out may seem quite a bit in advance, but it's necessary. You don't have to *hire* anyone this early, but you need to get them lined up. After all, you don't want to realize, the night before your opening, that you don't have a sales manager!

One of the first skills you must learn as an entrepreneur is to delegate. Figure out what tasks you can afford to have someone else take care of. In a small business, resources are always tight, so it's important to get the most out of them. The same is true of your employees. If you do not use your employees' full potential, you are wasting money. Pay as high a wage as you can and communicate with them up front about your long-term

217

goals. Nothing is worse than hiring an employee who leaves two months later because he really didn't see himself with your company long term.

Learn to treat your employees differently from one another. They are not all the same kind of person. You must communicate in a way in which each can hear you, so that you can achieve your goals through their work. If you hire relatives, this will take on even greater importance. Managing family can be tricky. The people closest to you may have trouble seeing you as the boss. In those cases you may need to overcommunicate until things gel.

EMERSON'S essentials

Different generations bring different attitudes toward work. In order to be an effective manager, you need to educate yourself on how to effectively communicate across ages as well as cultures.

What Kind of Employee Do You Want?

The obvious answer is the hardest-working, most conscientious individual you can find at the lowest possible cost. You want someone who is willing to work when you need her. First, though, you need to really understand the staffing needs of your business. Whether it be sales coverage for the hours you have the doors open, a delivery person, a helper, technical support staff, or someone to answer phones, you must know how many hours are involved, the skills required, and the duration of the position. These are keys to making the right hiring decision.

The Job Description

One of the first things you must do, once you have considered what kind of help you need, is to write a detailed job description. Write down everything the employee could possibly be asked to do, so she or he can be clear about how big the job is from the start. A good job description is key to helping an employee do her job effectively. It will also clearly communicate your expectations of job performance. You can also use the document as a basis for your job review.

- Create an exhaustive list of job tasks, then prioritize them. Try not to be overwhelming, just accurate.
- Divide the list into three categories: critical tasks, routine tasks, and occasional tasks.
- Keep your job description aspirational; your goal is to attract people who can think, not just complete tasks.

Once you have a job description, you must evaluate what kind of person you need to fulfill all these duties. There are several categories of employee that might meet your requirements:

Full Time

A full-time salaried employee who works a forty-hour week can receive overtime just like employees who are paid hourly, unless they are an exempt employee.

Exempt employees employed as executive, administrative, professional, and outside sales employees and certain computer employees may be considered exempt from both minimum wage and overtime pay. These are sometimes called "white collar" exemptions.

You must pay Social Security, disability, and federal and state taxes for all full-time and part-time employees. However, if you have under fifty employees, you have options as to whether you provide health, vacation, or retirement benefits. In many cases, the benefits you provide will depend on the labor pool you're hiring from. If the skill set you require of an employee is scarce, be prepared to offer competitive salary and benefit packages to attract the best talent.

Part Time

A part-time employee generally works from fifteen to thirty hours per week and can be a solid asset in covering hours such as nights and weekends, when your business might need to provide customer service support during off hours. Part-time help can provide great flexibility in meeting increased sales activity or addressing a surge in call volumes. Most importantly, part-time staffing permits you to adjust worker schedules to reflect the needs of your business. The primary downside is that you may be competing with their full-time positions and may not always get the hours you need from them. Generally, you do not have to pay either medical or retirement benefits to part-time employees, but this also depends on the skills you require and the state of the labor pool.

Temporary

A temporary worker, often hired through a staffing agency, can usually be on the job within a few hours, and can quickly help you meet an increase in business needs. Changing lifestyles and increased mobility in recent years have made temporary work very attractive to many highly skilled people. In many instances, temporary employees work from outside the office.

An agency can shorten the time and expense of recruiting, screening, interviewing, and checking on prospective employees. The major downside to using such employees is that their training and orientation is lost when that worker moves on. Additionally, these workers cost you a bit more than an hourly employee would. You also cannot expect the same level of loyalty or dedication to your business that you would from a permanent employee.

Contractors

These workers, known as freelancers or 1099 employees, can be very valuable in meeting your business needs, especially short-term complex ones, without adding to payroll. They work for a straight hourly rate and are responsible for their own payroll taxes. If you pay a contractor more than

$600 per year, you are required to send a 1099 tax form to them and to the IRS to report their income. You define the scope and timing of the project that you want done, negotiate the price, and specify the benchmarks.

Once the project is done, the contractor moves on. If you want to keep him on for a project expansion, you may have to renegotiate, and this could cost you. You can start off your employees as contractors on a project basis to see if you like their work style and performance. This will ease your budget since you won't have to pay benefits and taxes immediately, and you can get rid of problem employees before they can file for unemployment benefits.

Interns

College students working toward their degrees are often encouraged or required to participate in internship and co-op programs that relate to their field of study. This can be a low-cost source of labor for your company. In return for their labor, you give them college credits and experience in your business, and usually some pay. Most interns these days expect payment, and most intern programs require that employees offer at least minimum wage to the student workers.

You must create some ground rules, such as the length of time your intern must work per week. Establish a dress code: no jeans, sneakers, or piercings, etc. It's also good if you can give them a specific project to complete by the time they are finished with their internship. If you do this, whenever there's downtime they can work on that project. Try to assign projects that will test their skills, teach them new skills, and bring value to your business.

Internships occur during the school year or over summer or winter breaks. Co-op students are with the business a longer period of time. Many co-op students tend to be around for six months.

Providing internships and co-op opportunities is a great way of establishing working relationships with local colleges and key faculty members, which could also give you access to some low-cost consulting assistance.

The Selection Process

As the owner and sole employee of the business (for now), you are the personnel department and will have to decide whether the potential hire will be a help or a hindrance.

What kinds of skills do you expect to find in your potential hire? If you are looking for a salesperson and your candidate is not outgoing or seems wary of strangers, he may not be the best candidate. If you are looking for someone with technical skills in graphics or computer-aided design and she is unfamiliar with the programs and lingo associated with that profession, you may have a problem.

Like anything else in business, referrals for employees are useful. Send out job descriptions to everyone in your personal email database, to see if someone you know can send you a great candidate. Also use job listing websites including www.careerbuilder.com, www.craigslist.org, and www.upwork.com to find employees, and reach out to career services advisors for recent college graduates. A poor selection process costs you both time and money and can be unfair to the person you select.

In your job description, you've listed and prioritized the needed skills. The more interviews you conduct, the more you will be able to distinguish between those who are good at interviewing and those who are the best fit for your company.

The Employment Application

One great source of screening information is the application for employment that the candidate completes before the interview. Standard blank applications are available on the Internet.

Make sure the form you use includes space for the candidate to give his or her name, address, phone, and Social Security number; educational data for all schools attended, degrees, diplomas, and certifications; criminal background data, arrest records, or felony convictions; professional references with names, titles, and contact information; and prior employment details including the period of employment.

Going over these applications, you'll be able to easily reject the people whose skill sets don't match your requirements or who are unqualified for some other reason. From the remainder, select the best. They're your interview pool.

Ask the candidates who interview to sign forms giving your firm permission to check their credit report and/or perform a drug screening. The vendors who perform these services can provide the appropriate release forms.

The final step before the interviews is to prepare questions that will give you some insight into the personality and attitude of the candidates. The answers you get will really help you round out your impression of them.

Here are some questions and prompts you should cover:

- Tell me about your experience.
- Why did you apply for this job?
- What do you know about our company?
- What are your long-terms goals for your career?
- What do you see yourself doing five years from now?
- What is your most important accomplishment to date?
- What motivates you?
- Describe your favorite boss and your worst, and why.
- Why should I hire you?
- Have you ever had a conflict with a coworker? How did you resolve it?
- Describe a time when you had to multitask while handling a major project.
- Have you ever worked in a small business environment?

There are five things to keep in mind when conducting an interview:

1. Be a good listener.
2. Know how to redirect a conversation.

3. Take notes during the interview.
4. Go with your gut instinct (if something doesn't feel right, it's not right).
5. The candidate is also interviewing you, so be ready to answer questions.

Putting People on Payroll

Now that you're employing people, get ready for some serious record keeping. When you add employees you also add a paperwork burden to your business. You must make sure that you have W-2 forms (for all full-time and part-time employees) and W-9 forms (for all 1099 contract employees) updated annually. Use a payroll service to handle the payroll taxes—FICA, state taxes, Social Security deductions, disability contributions, and others. Talk with your accountant, lawyer, and/or payroll service before hiring anyone. Systems must be in place before you have employees working for you. You can go to jail faster for not paying payroll taxes than for not paying income taxes.

Payroll Companies

A great source of help in making your hiring process compliant with the law is to use a payroll company. You need a firm that pays your employees, your payroll taxes, and files your tax forms on time. Some factors to consider when choosing a company are:

- **Cost:** It could cost $40–$350 per payroll depending on how many people you have using the service. Don't overpay for services you don't need (e.g., HR consulting or benefits management). Shop around, and ask for referrals from other business owners.
- **Responsiveness:** If there is a mistake with payroll, how quickly can it be corrected and paychecks be reissued?

- **Communication:** How hard is it for the company to add a new employee to your system? Updating the payroll list should be quick and easy.
- **Technology:** Do they offer a web platform to submit payroll data?

You will need to communicate with the payroll service regularly, so make sure they have qualified personnel to work with you.

EMERSON'S experience

One time my regular payroll clerk was on vacation, and her replacement accidentally processed a $50,000 paycheck for me. Nearly $28,000 in taxes was also pulled from my account, and it took me a week to get it straightened out. Shortly after, I switched payroll companies.

Ask for small business references and check them. Make sure the company is bonded and registered with the Better Business Bureau.

Basic monthly payroll services include paycheck processing, online account access, quarterly tax filings, and direct deposit. Prices can range depending on the frequency of payroll and the number of employees. Per-check fees, if applicable, range from $2–$5 or more, and additional fees for adding new employees, check delivery, and extra reporting are typical. Make sure you get a full breakdown of all fees before you commit to a provider.

Offering Benefits

Next, you must define what benefits you are prepared to offer a new employee. Generally, the lower the employee rank, the lower the salary and the fewer the benefits. What you pay for employees is defined by the skills, experience, and education they have, as well as by what the competition is offering. Figure into your cost any perks you offer (free/subsidized education, paid sick time, numerous vacation days, rapid advancement, 401(k), etc.). The benefits you offer reflect the importance you place on attracting the right people. If you run a home healthcare agency, you won't hire any registered nurses for minimum wage. But if you are looking for a sales clerk, you may be able to start with a lower rate. Make sure you have a good idea of what you will need to pay to get the talent you need.

What if you can't offer competitive benefits? How can you attract good help? One possibility is to offer potential employees the opportunity to share in the company's profits through direct stock ownership. Another possibility is a bonus program that will benefit everyone if certain goals are met.

EMERSON'S essentials

Stay-at-home moms looking to get back into the workforce appreciate flexibility. Offering adaptable work schedules and virtual work can be a big incentive to qualified workers. Other possibilities include a compressed workweek—four nine-hour days, or three twelve-hour days, for example.

Job Sharing and Gig Workers

Job sharing is also a great way to get the help you need—two permanent part-time employees share one position. If you operate a customer service–based business, this may be a great solution to get a high-quality employee at a reasonable cost. HireMyMom.com is a great resource to hire stay-at-home moms with great skills who left the workforce to focus on raising their kids and are ready to get back into the workforce.

Consider hiring virtual gig workers, consultants, or freelancers. The gig economy is one of the most important tools for small businesses to find talent. In 2020, more than one-third of US workers participated in the gig economy. That's nearly fifty-nine million Americans who are available for temporary, flexible job opportunities.

High-speed Internet, email, Dropbox, Slack, Zoom, Google Meet, Skype, Microsoft Teams, Google Workspace, teleconferencing, overnight mail, and same-day courier services have made the virtual office seamless. There are a few things to consider prior to scouting for a virtual gig worker. The first step is to do an internal assessment. Is this a project-based job or an ongoing operation function in your business? Project-based work is easier to manage using gig workers. If the work you need done is an ongoing key function in your business, be careful not to get into worker misclassification. The Department of Labor and the Internal Revenue Service have strict guidelines on what is considered a contract worker versus employee status.

Develop a list of qualifications for the ideal candidate, and know exactly what you need the person to do, your monthly budget, and your timeline to get started. It's important to be up front about whether this is a short-term or long-term opportunity.

Visit your potential gig worker's website to view their portfolio and see if they have testimonials. Ask them to email samples of their work or provide case studies of previous assignments. Check their LinkedIn profile. Do they have any recommendations? Pay attention to what types of projects a candidate has listed in their profile. Review their work and decide if they can produce or execute what you need. Ask them for references and check them. Then, schedule a conversation. This informal mini-interview should take place over Zoom, the phone, or WhatsApp. A face-to-face meeting is best. Speaking to the person face-to-face establishes a personal connection. You'll get a feel for their personality; see if you click or clash; and assess their commitment to their craft. Prior to the call, make a list of a few questions that speak to their skills, their interest in your project, and their commitment to working with your company. You also want to clarify their communication skills and determine if they'll be able to follow your instructions and participate in any meetings with the rest of your team.

If you feel good about the person, give him or her a test project to find out if there is a fit. It can be an aspect of a larger project or a completely different project, and you should pay for the work performed.

Some of the best websites to source gig workers include LinkedIn, Upwork, Fiverr, Toptal.com, and Liveops.

Managing a Remote Workforce

Once you've built your remote workforce of gig workers, how do you manage them? Here are five steps to take:

1. **Communicate your goals and mission clearly.** Effective communication is the bread and butter of successful remote work. Only when you can communicate with your team members with utmost transparency and convey the goals with clarity can you lead your team to succeed.

2. **Use project management and scheduling software.** Technology is the enabler of successful remote work. Staying informed of everyone's schedules and assigning tasks so that everyone is clear on deliverables and timelines is imperative. When the information is centralized and everyone's aware of schedules and workload, chances of efficient and smart use of resources are much higher. Consider project management tools like Zoho Projects, Asana, ActiveCollab, Project.co, Trello, and Basecamp.

3. **Use the right collaboration tools to get the work done.** You will also need file sharing, version control, and customer relationship management (CRM) tools. You must give your team the right tools, and train yourself and your team on how to use them. When you first start out, you'll be buying apps to set up your back office; make sure you understand how they integrate

with other tools you are using. Learn how to log in to all of your apps so you can check on your team. My best software recommendations: Dropbox, Google Drive, Slack, Pipedrive, Mixmax, Nimble, and WeTransfer.

4. **Foster inclusivity.** Companies with a diverse workforce need to ensure that everyone (gig workers; different genders and generations; and everyone regardless of ethnicity, race, sexual orientation, or disability) meets regularly, feels connected, works as a team, and is given equal opportunities to thrive. I host a weekly staff meeting every Monday at 4 p.m. to make sure everyone is on the same page and feels connected to the team.

5. **Build rapport among your team.** Celebrate birthdays and weddings as a team. Form a book club with your employees. Mail everyone an inspirational book, then schedule a lunch-and-learn session a month later; provide lunch for everyone, no matter where they are, and let everyone give feedback on the book, even your interns. Get the whole team together in person at least once a year for a retreat so that everyone can get to know each other socially as well as in business.

Creating the Rules

Every business has rules, which need to be explained to all employees so everyone understands your expectations. You should establish policies on insubordination, lateness, laziness, excessive absenteeism, lying, theft, substance abuse, personal use of cell phones, and other personality issues. It is a good idea to ask new employees to sign a noncompete/nondisclosure agreement and their employee handbook as proof they understand your business practices and grounds for termination. This cuts down on any confusion later and gives you legal protection in the event you have to fire an employee.

EMERSON'S experience

In the early days of my business, I could not always pay my employees, but to make up for it I allowed my staff to use my equipment and resources to do freelance work for other people. I also bought lunch and dinner every day (largely because we worked most nights until 9 p.m. or so). I would give them subway and bus tokens or rides home from work every night. Whenever it was somebody's birthday, I always bought that person a nice gift. At the end of a hard contract, we would all go out to dinner at a nice restaurant with spouses and significant others.

I also allowed everyone to interview any potential hires. They all voted on any new hire, and the vote had to be unanimous before an offer was made, even for our interns. My rationale for this was that my core staff was the priority, and if a new person was going to disrupt the office vibe, they could not join the "family."

Reprimanding Your Employees

One of the hardest things to do in business is reprimand a member of the staff. Have any corrective conversations in a private setting. Start by listing several positives before addressing the negative incident. I also make a point of highlighting anything I could have done differently that would have made the situation better. We can all learn something in any situation.

Hiring Family Members

Hiring family members may be your best source of inexpensive labor, but the trade-offs can be dedication and attitude. The separation between work and your personal life can erode quickly, and both can suffer if the demands of your work leave no time for your personal priorities. Whether you are employing siblings, spouse, children, parents, cousins, or even very close friends, business conflicts can put enormous strain on relationships.

Spouses and siblings working together need clearly defined roles. They should drive separate cars and have offices away from each other.

It's important that relatives be treated like everyone else in terms of pay and job title so that everything in your business can work together harmoniously. The best approach to minimize the inevitable pressures that result from working with family is communication, communication, and more communication.

The website www.familybusinessmatters.consulting provides excellent insight into problems and solutions for family-managed businesses. Many of these solutions are low-cost or free.

Dealing with Lateness

Be sure to have a policy regarding attendance and your business's core hours. At the same time, this is another area in which you need flexibility. If you dock pay for every fifteen minutes of tardiness and give people a hard time when they need time off, chances are they'll call in sick on the day you need them the most. You can be flexible as long as you know what is going on.

EMERSON'S experience

There is honor in all work, so treat all employees with respect. Without them, your business would be in peril. Whenever I introduce a staff member to a client or anyone else, I say the employee works with me and not for me. It sounds better and is more accurate. I also empower my staff to give me feedback constantly. If I do something they find objectionable, I invite them to let me know.

One key thing I took away from my days in corporate America was: People leave people, not jobs. Your staff is an extension of you. Be good to them. Treat them like family—although we all know that nobody's family is perfect.

EMERSON'S essentials

If you treat people like employees, that is how they will act. If you nickel and dime people, they will do the same to you and to your business. Your employees will be more concerned about lunchtime or what time they get off than what you are paying them to do and do well. Whenever you hire anyone—even an intern—it's a good idea to give him or her a copy of your business plan. If you can get all of your staff to buy into what you're trying to do, they will be more understanding when money is tight or when everyone needs to work until midnight to complete a project.

It's Just Not Working Out

Firing someone is a high-stress situation because often—though not always—it signals that you have made a bad hiring decision. When your employee has not met your expectations or doesn't fit into your organization, it is time to say goodbye.

When an employee is terminated, it is usually for one of two reasons—an immediate firing for insubordination, theft, drug use, or illegal activity, or an ongoing behavior termination. Reasons for the latter could include chronic lateness, laziness, high absenteeism, incompetence, or poor attitude.

Both types of firings present legal challenges, which is why you should document their cause in detail.

1. **Immediate firing:** Document the specific behavior that is the cause of termination—when it occurred, where, and who witnessed it (if possible), and cite the specific passages in your company handbook or code of conduct that it violates.

2. **Ongoing behavior:** Note each instance of the behavior that is grounds for the termination. Document that you asked the employee for specific improvements and note the time frame in which these were to be met. The time you set can be a week, a month, or more depending on how serious you consider the problem.

Your documentation can help you significantly if the employee files a lawsuit or you need to fight a claim for unemployment.

When informing the employee of your decision to terminate his or her relationship with your company, stick to the facts. Don't show emotion—even though you'll probably be feeling it. Terminate with kindness and in privacy. Arrange for the employee to return all company property, including keys and IDs.

Regardless of how employees leave your organization, whether voluntarily or involuntarily, you should always conduct an exit interview. The exit interview should be calm and professional. Details of the interview are important, so carefully note each point made in the discussion. Every time an employee leaves your organization, try to learn something you can do better.

EMERSON'S action steps

1. Write a detailed job description to clarify what skills you need.
2. Create an employee handbook so everyone knows the rules.
3. Hire a payroll service to keep things simple.
4. Tread lightly when hiring family members. You could lose your business and the relationship.
5. Keep a paper trail on all disciplinary meetings with staff.
6. If an employee doesn't work out, consider what role you played in his failure.

CHAPTER 17

SET UP CUSTOMER SERVICE SYSTEMS

Before you generate your first sale, you need to think about customer service. What are your customer service policies going to be? Are all sales final, will you issue store credit, or will you offer a money-back guarantee on your product or service? All businesses must have a customer service policy for telephone or email inquiries.

You must train your staff in how to greet and assist customers, and all employees need to know how to handle unhappy customers. In these days of increasing global competition, customer service can provide your competitive edge.

Companies that are focused on building long-term relationships know what customers need, want, and expect. This is the core benefit of excellent customer service. Your competitors will bombard your best customers with reasons they should drop your company and start doing business with them: lower costs for comparable service, a wider array of services for the same cost, or the use of newer technologies. But if you provide good customer service, you'll be able to retain your customer base.

Why is this important? Keeping existing customers is cheaper than trying to get new ones. A recent survey published by Accenture reported that 59 percent of customers surveyed switched at least one service provider due to poor service.

Cost is not everything. Customers want their needs taken care of, and often they're willing to pay a bit more for better service. Outstanding customer service can also be your unique value proposition. Think Zappos: They sell shoes, clothing, handbags, accessories, and more, but what made them a marquee brand was providing the very best customer service, customer experience, and company culture. They have built their success by treating all their customers like VIPs.

EMERSON'S experience

When I was kid, my dad worked a second job as a part-time salesman at Sears. One year around Christmastime a man, who looked like he had worked all day on a construction site, walked into the electronics department. The man was dirty and muddy and still had his work boots on. My dad noticed that no one was waiting on him. Clearly the other salespeople had made assumptions about this customer based on how he looked.

This was back in the 1980s, when camcorders had just come on the market. The man wanted to see how those new machines worked. My dad did a full demonstration and even moved the machine so the man could see himself on TV in the showroom.

At the end of the demonstration the man said, "I'm not going to buy anything tonight. I want my wife to see this too. When is the next time you'll be working?"

When my dad clocked in the following Sunday, the man and his wife were waiting for him—this time cleaned up and smartly dressed. After another demonstration, the man bought ten camcorders. It turned out he owned a construction company. He bought a camcorder for every member of his family for Christmas.

It wasn't only his family that had a good holiday. My dad's commission on that sale was $1,500. That night Dad sat my brothers and me down and told us never to judge a book by its cover and to always treat everyone with respect. That was my first customer service lesson.

Underpromise and Overdeliver

Delivering more than what you promised is a good way to build customer rapport—both outside and inside your company. Likewise, doing it sooner than expected makes a strong impression.

EMERSON'S experience

Successful companies make a habit of exceeding customer expectations. I recently took my car into the dealership to get an oil change, and to check out an interior light that was not working properly. The service area was crowded that day, and I expected at least a two hour wait. To my surprise, not only did the service people do the oil change; they also replaced the bulb and put in new windshield wipers (I had asked the service advisor to "take a look at the wipers for me")—all in an hour! Best of all, the wipers and light were done at no charge. They did more than I expected, and I could not have been more pleased. The dealership created a positive link between their brand and me and reinforced the customer relationship. I'll remember this experience when I buy my next car.

Solve Your Customer's Problem

If you can't identify your customer's problem, you won't solve it. Worse, you will waste time and lose credibility. You must describe the problem clearly, and do it from the customer's point of view. To find out what the problem is, ask the right questions and listen before you act. Here are some approaches that are very effective:

- **Ask the customer what would solve the problem.** Many times their requests can be surprisingly reasonable and relatively inexpensive. If the cause of the problem is clearly your product's failure, refund the customer's money or replace the item.
- **Eighty percent of Americans believe that lack of courtesy is a problem in the United States.** By focusing on basic courtesy with your employees you can set yourself apart from the competition, especially since so many potential customers are not accustomed to it.
- **Be flexible.** Even if you know a customer's complaint is suspect, negotiate with him or her perhaps for partial credit toward a replacement purchase or a reduced-price or complimentary service. Reduce the areas of conflict that keep you from getting to an amicable solution.

EMERSON'S essentials

In business, it's cheaper to keep the customer. Do not argue with customers about their opinion. It's bad for your blood pressure and bad for business. And in the long run, you won't win.

The last and least attractive option in any customer dialogue is to just say no—but sometimes you have to do it. Managing difficult customers is part of the territory when you open a business. When it seems like nothing that you do is right, forget about preserving the relationship—preserve your sanity instead. If you have a client who just won't be satisfied, no matter what you do, let him go. Work hard to save the relationships that you can. Take great care of customers who love your work and acknowledge your dedication and professionalism. They are the backbone of your long-term business success.

Request Customer Feedback

Collecting customer feedback to measure customer satisfaction with your company's performance is a way for you to proactively get information on how a customer values your products and services. You should reach out to customers within seven to ten days of providing service. It's a good idea to ask for a review on Tripadvisor, Yelp, or OpenTable when you are reaching out to your customers. Satisfaction surveys are the most accurate barometers to predict the success of a company because they directly ask customers about the critical success factors of your business. If done effectively, satisfaction surveys can deliver powerful insights and provide ways to gain a competitive edge. When measuring customer satisfaction, you can gather critical feedback with questions such as these:

- How satisfied are you with the purchase you made?
- How satisfied are you with the service you received?
- How likely are you to buy from us again?

Most surveys ask customers to rate their experiences in these areas on a numbered scale. With enough feedback from your customers, you can get a pretty good idea about how you are doing. If the results are not good, you've got work to do. See the Sample Customer Satisfaction Survey at the end of this book.

EMERSON'S action steps

1. Treat your customers well, and they will not only follow you; they will also sell for you by sharing their experience with others.
2. Know your customer's needs, wants, and motives.
3. Don't argue with your customers. You can't win.
4. Work hard to save the relationships that you can. A bad reputation travels fast.
5. Make sure you and your staff treat all your customers with courtesy. Even something this simple can set you apart from the competition.
6. Use customer feedback to make changes and improve your business.

PART III
Go!

CHAPTER 18

LAUNCHING YOUR BUSINESS

One Month Before You Start

You have been extremely busy assembling all of the elements to get your business started—the idea, the support, the financing, the location, the marketing plan—and most of all, nurturing your confidence to make it all happen. As with any big plan, there are usually details that must be addressed at the last minute. You don't want a small issue to prevent or delay your launch.

Here is a list of the top twenty items to check on in the weeks leading up to your launch. Make sure your bases are covered before your opening day.

❏ I've registered for an EIN number with the IRS and opened a business bank account.
❏ I've obtained required business licenses and permits and checked on zoning regulations.

- ❏ I've set up a business filing system.
- ❏ I've purchased a fireproof safe to store checks, software, and critical documents.
- ❏ I've ordered collateral materials, all of which have my logo and contact information on them.
- ❏ I've purchased a supply of business forms such as sales slips, order forms, and blank receipts.
- ❏ I've purchased or leased and set up all the equipment I'll need—e.g., point of sale (POS) system, cash register, copier/scanner, computers, color printer, postage meter, etc.
- ❏ I've established an on-call agreement with a technology consultant.
- ❏ I've hired a lawyer to draft templates for contract agreements, mutual nondisclosure agreements, etc.
- ❏ I've hired a bookkeeper or accountant to set up accounting software and provide monthly support.
- ❏ I've conducted background checks and bonding on anyone handling money or merchandise.
- ❏ I've made sure phone lines are operating and voice-mail greetings are recorded.
- ❏ I've set up payment processing via Square or PayPal.
- ❏ I've carried out an orientation for my employees on how to use the POS system and process credit cards and returns.
- ❏ I've made up and distributed weekly/monthly employee work schedules.
- ❏ I've sent out invitations to a grand opening event.
- ❏ I've set up a website with an online merchant service account to accept payments.
- ❏ I've launched online advertising or direct mail locally.
- ❏ I've got a presence on Instagram, LinkedIn, Facebook, Twitter, YouTube, Pinterest, and any other useful social media sites where I can spread the word about my business.
- ❏ I've made sure news releases announcing the launch are ready to send to local media and publish on the website.

Go through this list and make sure you've put a check next to each item. If need be, push back the date of your opening to give yourself time to get all your ducks lined up. While it's not good to delay the opening of your business, it's far worse to open with tasks left undone. Those skipped items will come back to haunt you in the weeks and months to come if you neglect them now.

Getting the Basics Right

The list is primarily concerned with the launch of your business. But as we've seen, there are other things that have more to do with the day-to-day running of your business. You also need to do the following:

- **Set up your customer service system.** Make sure your employees are aware of how to handle unhappy customers. Do your people have the power to make a customer refund, or do all adjustments need to be made by you? Having a clear set of rules up front will make your job easier.
- **Manage the money.** Use accounting software to track all sales, invoices, receipts, and any payroll. You should also keep physical copies of all receipts, invoices, and canceled checks. Set up a shredder to destroy credit card information to prevent theft or fraud. The system for managing your finances should make it easy to see income and expenses monthly and ease the creation of tax documents.
- **Firm up your vendor relationships.** If you are selling services and your business experiences rapid growth, you can use temporary help such as freelancers, consultants, or interns, or you can expand the hours of your staff. However, if you are selling a product and there is a dramatic rise in demand, you may need your suppliers to extend enough credit to help you meet it. Keep your suppliers in the loop about your needs and pay them as promptly as you can. The key to building a solid vendor relationship is early, frequent, and up-front communication.

- **Get your employee mix right.** Unless you are a solopreneur, your employees will be critical to your business success. To get the best employees, carefully look at their work habits, enthusiasm, attitude, reliability, knowledge, and common sense. A good hiring decision can save you grief once the doors are open and your business has launched. It's also a good habit to already know your next hire for every position in your business.
- **Create an emergency plan.** You should have an idea of who will run the business if you get sick or have to pull away from it for an extended time. Would you have to close shop, or do you have someone who could step in until you come back? What is your "plan B"?

In the month before you launch, review these lists several times. You've spent twelve months getting to this place. Avoid any last-minute stumbles as you prepare for the greatest adventure of your life.

It's Go Time!

When you launch a business the most important thing you must do is attract customers and generate leads. With that as the goal, when you created your marketing plan you developed a content strategy. This process included deciding what social media vehicles and online advertising to use for your business launch.

For some businesses, certain advertising strategies aren't cost-effective and don't make sense. Based on your target market, it is important to use the most appropriate advertising options.

Launch Strategies

Let's break down different launch strategies for generating sales leads and getting customers in the door.

Professional Service Businesses

If you are a professional service business, attracting clients is all about the face-to-face meetings. Host an open house if you have professional office space.

Often professional service businesses sell solutions, which means a significant amount of time is spent up front understanding the challenge faced by a prospective customer. Lawyers, doctors, accountants, creative services firms, and technology firms are these types of enterprises.

At the start of your business, the work you've done in the previous year networking will be key. Call on your network to spread the word of your launch. Send emails to existing contacts. Schedule Zoom meetings to do capabilities presentations. If your launch coincides with a trade show, consider distributing your marketing materials there, to announce that your company has entered the market. Set up lunch and dinner meetings prior to arriving at the show with target customers. The key thing to remember is that timely follow-up after the meetings is essential to growing relationships.

EMERSON'S essentials

Never rent a booth the first year you attend a trade show. Attending trade shows is expensive enough. Make sure that you are going to get a bang for your buck before you shell out cash to rent booth space. Walk the show the first year, talk to exhibitors about their success rate, and make sure your target market potential is worth the investment.

Online Businesses

Generating buzz for your new business with a social media marketing campaign is key. Six months before you launch, you should increase your visibility on one or two social sites where your target customers spend time. It could be Twitter, LinkedIn, YouTube, Instagram, Pinterest, or Facebook. Once you are at your launch time you should be even more visible. Set up a fact of the day about your industry or service. Use services like Buffer, Hootsuite, or Sprout Social to schedule daily social media promotions.

EMERSON'S essentials

Always remember the 6-4-1-1 rule on social media. For every six postings, four should be to educate or entertain, one should be a soft sell, and one should be a hard sell, directly promoting your product or service.

- Create an event on Facebook to invite your network to your grand opening event.
- Have a site-warming party online to launch your website or e-commerce store. Facebook and Twitter are great for this. To attract visitors and bring awareness to your new business, use a thirty-day giveaway program and guest bloggers. You can also pull this off with a Zoom event.
- Comment on other blogs and participate in online forums to get attention.
- Post a launch video for your audience on all social sites and use it to launch your YouTube channel.
- Send out social media press releases as well as traditional news releases.
- Purchase pay-per-click advertising. Businesses typically bid for ads on Facebook or LinkedIn, or they bid on keyword phrases relevant to their target market. Google Ads is the largest ad network operator. Depending on the size of your marketing budget this could be a good move. You can be there instantly to solve the need of the potential customers. The most important thing is to have the right keywords to attract the right customers.

Retail Businesses

Success in retail is all about attracting a high volume of walk-in customers. As you launch your local retail business focus on providing neighborhood convenience, creating a unique shopping experience, and offering personalized merchandise focused on the needs of your target customers. Make sure your website is mobile ready, with store hours displayed, and that mobile visitors see exactly what's being offered on the website. Here are some more retail promotion ideas:

- Offer special opening day discounts and specials gifts to attract clients.
- Hire teens to hand out flyers.
- Partner with the other businesses in your area to do co-branded activities.
- Take out an ad on the table placemat at the local diner in your neighborhood.
- Put a coupon in the community discount mailer or clipper magazine; a well-placed local mobile search ad in your area can be effective as well.
- Try Facebook ads in the specific zip codes you serve.
- Have the radio station do a live broadcast from your location.

For Any Business

Whether you're launching a consulting operation, an online business, or a neighborhood store, here are some things you can do to draw attention to your new business:

Host a Grand Opening

Offer giveaways and games for the entire family. Schedule a live remote with a local radio station that serves your target market. Offer great opening day specials and discount coupons for a return visit.

Develop a Membership Program

Create a frequent buyers club. Offer special sales, shopping hours, and special discounts. Sponsor a special event, e.g., a ballet or ball game to which customers get VIP tickets.

Host a Site-Warming Party Online

Feature a countdown to your opening prominently on your home page. Host a live event on Facebook or Instagram with giveaways to drive traffic to your new website. If you have a blog, develop a series of posts specifically about your launch and any special offers.

Become a PR Machine

If you can't afford to hire a publicist for the launch, do it yourself. You need to have a contact list for regional and national media. Develop three hooks to pitch your business to the media and don't forget the local business journal. Try one of these ideas:

- Create an exceptional guarantee.
- Try a sports gimmick, e.g., the company president will shave his head if the local football team wins.
- Develop a special sale item for the opening week, with a portion of the proceeds going to charity.
- Invite the community in. Hire musicians to play in your store every Friday for a few months after the launch.
- Throw some sort of contest for college students to create a jingle for the store or a YouTube video.
- Shoot TikTok videos of people dancing to fun music while wearing your items.

The day your business opens its doors will be one of unparalleled excitement for you. Be sure to get a good night's sleep, because you're about to embark on a road that will be filled with long days and sometimes longer nights. But at the end is the incredible reward of becoming your own boss.

CHAPTER 19

YOUR LEADERSHIP MATTERS

After You Start

There's a misconception that, because you're a small business owner, you're automatically a leader. While it's true that you may be a leader in terms of influencing sales, there is so much more to leadership than convincing people to buy from you.

Leadership really starts with your ability to lead yourself, and the longer you run your business, the better you will become at being a leader as your business grows.

If you're like many entrepreneurs, you got into your business because you had experience or passion for something. Maybe you run a bakery specializing in gluten-free desserts because as a child you loved baking with your mom. Perhaps you inherited your parents' dry-cleaning business and have been working in it since you were a teen. Or maybe you stumbled into entrepreneurship by giving handmade items as holiday gifts, and people started asking you if they could buy them.

Whatever the "thing" is that you love doing, it probably does not include leading others. Leadership is a learned skill. First, you learn to lead yourself, and then you learn to lead others.

Panicking yet? Not to worry. Entrepreneurship is the best personal development tool on the planet. If you feel ill-equipped to lead well today, that's okay. Start where you are. There are things you can do to boost your leadership skills, and if you're in business long enough, leadership will become second nature to you.

What Is Leadership?

A leader is any person who is in a position of influence. This can be anyone—a parent, a car salesperson, a media personality, an intern, or a high school teacher. The fundamental skills that make a good leader are the same. The best leaders:

- Have the ability to develop a vision and inspire others
- Set clear goals, stay focused, and communicate well
- Give and receive feedback
- Know the strengths and weaknesses of themselves and teammates
- Know when to ask for outside help
- Are approachable, honest, and committed
- Know how to successfully execute a strategy

Having any of these skills can lead to some form of success, but you will need all of these skills in order to run your small business effectively. One of the things you'll need to consider is your leadership style.

Leadership Style and Why It Matters

Think back to the bosses you've had in the past. Did they rule with an iron fist, constantly looking for errors in your work? Or were they more trusting and willing to let you do your job without them micromanaging you? Were they organized and thoughtful, providing ample time to accomplish tasks? Did they include everyone in the decision-making processes of the business? Did they do everything in a last-minute and haphazard way, expecting you to quickly fall in line behind their every whim?

Every leader has a unique leadership style, and this style is translated into the culture of the business—for better or for worse. If a leader is empathetic and organized, an office environment is probably similarly situated. If a leader is bossy and uncaring, chances are good that the people under his leadership are bossy and mean-spirited as well.

The good news is that you have a choice. You can be the crazed and helter-skelter leader, or you can be the good-natured and organized leader. Just know that the tone you set for yourself will be the one you set for your team and other stakeholders. Let's take a look at seven leadership styles. Do you see yourself in any of them?

The Seven Leadership Styles

Of the many leadership styles identified over the years, these seven stand out. Most were outlined by author Daniel Goleman. The best leaders know how to adjust their leadership style to the situation. Let's review the typical leadership varieties.

Visionary

The visionary leader can see the future. She inspires her staff with big-picture ideas to move the company forward. She mobilizes people to make changes or push toward that vision, but she doesn't dictate how they get there. Her enthusiasm is infectious.

Coaching

The coaching leader prioritizes communication and empowers employees to accomplish professional goals. It's not always about work. He makes an effort to get to know people on a personal level and build trust with them.

Affiliative

The affiliative leader focuses on her team members. She believes there should be a sense of community and cohesion among employees, and she works to create harmony. She values employees' emotional needs and quickly works to resolve conflicts between employees.

Democratic

The democratic leader gives everyone a voice. Decisions aren't made from on high; instead, they happen through consensus and collaboration. This leader knows how to take all employees' ideas into consideration.

Pacesetting

A pacesetting leader expects the best from his team and demonstrates by example exactly how he wants his team to perform. He's not a micro-manager but expects his employees to meet or exceed goals. He has high expectations; he demands them of himself and everyone else.

Coercive

The coercive leader uses iron fist leadership with employees. And while she can instill fear to elicit fast change, it may come at the price of her employees, who may wither under the pressure. These kinds of leaders have a high churn of employees.

Commanding

A commanding leader is one who sets the goals, determines the processes, and oversees all steps it takes to reach those goals with little or no input from team members. This is the perfect leader for any sort of crisis.

Identifying Your Leadership Style

Now that you've discovered the seven leadership styles, which resonates with you? You may find that you are a combination of two or three of them. For example, you may be a great visionary, but instead of gently leading your team to fulfill your vision, you bark orders at them and expect them to fall in line immediately. If you're not sure how to characterize yourself, look at your day-to-day interactions with people. Do you spend time asking them about their families and personal interests, or do you dive into work without any regard for their personal well-being? Do you instantly spot discord between two coworkers and make an effort to resolve it, or do you say or do things to fan the flames?

Do you know how to inspire your team to work their best toward a common goal? Do you take their ideas seriously and even implement them, or do you send the message that it's your way or the highway?

These questions can help you uncover which leadership style you use in managing your team and other stakeholders. As you evaluate your style, remember that it is within your power to change it. (Remember that it is a work in progress, and you will improve as you go!)

What Your Team and Others Expect from You As a Leader

Now that you have some ideas about different leadership styles, how do you think you stack up? Regardless of your leadership style, your team and stakeholders need certain things from you. Let's look at some concrete areas where your ability to lead could make a huge difference in your personal productivity and that of your team.

Be a Visionary

You'll have more success in your business if your vision is clear and you empower people to get invested in your vision. You must make your vision useful and important to people other than yourself. Creating a written document for your vision is helpful, but it is more impactful with visuals to showcase where you will be going with your business. In any case, your number one job is conveying your vision to others.

Make sure that whatever the finished piece you're putting your vision into only takes about two minutes to observe, read, and understand. From here, develop a two-minute description that you can recite that conveys the vision for your business. This should be your "elevator pitch." The idea is that if you were in an elevator ride with someone who could potentially help your business, you would be ready with your two-minute well-delivered description of your business, which would convince this person of why they should be interested in your business.

Communicate Clearly and Regularly

In order to communicate clearly, you first need to acknowledge that different people understand ideas better through different mediums and methods. Some people will learn better through lectures, written instruction, one-on-one instruction, visualization, or hands-on approaches. It's helpful to recognize first which methods you learn and understand best from. In addition to communicating well, it is critical that you communicate regularly. Your team does not want to find out about important changes after they happen, no matter how clearly you communicate them. The most effective leaders hold regular staff meetings and are transparent about what is happening in the business.

Do you understand instructions better when they are written or presented through a one-on-one tutorial? Perhaps it's through a combination of methods such as lectures and then hands-on approaches. Here's a quick way to determine what style of learning may work best for your team. Ask them these questions:

When consuming content from the Internet, which of the following do you prefer:

- Reading an article
- Listening to a podcast
- Watching a video
- Looking at an infographic
- Experimenting with a technique and then discussing it on a message board or social media

Once you know how you learn best to communicate, it's easy to see that others, such as employees and partners, will need different channels for communication.

Start by offering instructions and descriptions through both written and verbal communication.

Listen Well

If you want to become a better leader, then become a better listener. Stop thinking about what you're going to say while the other person is talking.

Instead of thinking about what you are going to say, think of key points that the other person brings up that you would like to hear more about. Make it a habit to use your turn in a conversation to ask a question about what the other person has said, instead of stating your own opinion. This is called "active listening."

This communication strategy helps develop rapport very quickly. Not only will the person feel more connected to you, but you most likely will understand what it is this person is trying to say. Remember, you already know what you're thinking, so your first goal should be to understand what the other person is thinking. This is especially important when dealing with dissatisfied customers. It creates a better impression of you in the eyes of the other people in the conversation when you are actively listening to them. If someone has a concern, even if you don't offer a solution, simply inquiring about the concern will make you appear compassionate in their mind. If you get someone to talk a lot about their favorite hobby, that person will associate the good feelings of his or her favorite hobby with you.

Receive Criticism Gracefully

In order to be more effective at giving and receiving feedback you must invite the customers to provide feedback. Time is valuable, so look at honest feedback as a gift. There are two important channels for feedback when running a business. The first channel is from the customer to you. The second channel is from your employees and partners to you. This second channel goes both ways, with you also providing feedback to employees and partners.

How to Receive Customer Feedback

It's important that you have an easy way for customers to voice their feedback about your product or service—whether it is praise or criticism. One of the biggest innovations that Amazon provided in customer relationships is the reviews section on products. Here, customers can voice their praise and criticism of a product.

You can solicit feedback with something as simple as a message box on your website that customers can fill out and immediately send to you, or it can be a Facebook page that customers can post on. The more easily customers can get their opinion to you, the better. In fact, being accessible to customer feedback is a hallmark of good customer service. Simply being available for immediate feedback may turn some customers' sour opinions more favorable.

You also need to consider whether this feedback should be public or private. In the case of Amazon, Yelp reviews, and Facebook pages, the feedback is public. This may seem scary because all other customers can see the criticism you may be facing, but they may also see the praise that you receive. In addition to this, customers can see how you handle a bad user experience. Did you offer an immediate refund and apologize for any bad experiences? Or did you get crabby and insist all transactions are final?

If you're not sure what the feedback will be like for your product or service, this will help you refine your products and service delivery. Also, if you get good feedback, you can always ask the customer if you can quote them as a testimonial on your website at a later date.

How to Give and Receive Feedback from Employees

If you really want your team to respect you, allow them to criticize you, and respond with grace. You need to schedule and maintain regular staff meetings. Your team may be hesitant to criticize you, but if you can understand how your leadership style is impacting them, you can create psychological safety, and they will share. And realize that each employee may respond differently to the same leadership style, so you may need to customize it based on the individual employee you are dealing with. If the meetings aren't regular, then the chances are that you will only call the team together to dramatically change course. This will create disarray and destroy productivity and morale. Even if things are going well, you should have the regularly scheduled meeting.

EMERSON'S essentials

Keep your feedback factual, not emotional. Both positive and critical feedback should always relate back to the company goals. The best way to determine what to say is to ask yourself, "How does this put us closer to our goals?" Did an employee move you closer or further from your vision? Tell them!

Remember, too, that your employees are assets you need in order to achieve your vision. If there is something that you're doing that is deterring them from their goals, then you need to recognize that. Some employees may be hesitant to provide you with feedback. Try asking the following questions in a one-on-one session:

- What do you hear others (e.g., competitors, customers, prospects, anonymous colleagues) saying about our company?
- What do you like the most about your job and what do you like the least?
- What would you do if you were in my position?

Encourage Creativity

Today's employees are looking for more than just a paycheck; they want an opportunity to be creative and grow professionally. Micromanagers don't leave room for employees to find creative solutions to problems, and organizations that don't foster creativity tend to see higher turnover. Consider how creative you let your staff get. Do you give them an assignment and leave the "how" up to them, or do you dictate exactly how a task should be done? If it's the latter, consider trusting your employees to find the best way for them to complete a task.

Be a Role Model

Don't underestimate your influence on your employees, for better or worse. As a leader, people look to you and may find inspiration, if you're willing to provide it. Do you have employees who would like to run their own business one day? Or those who are interested in tasks or roles you have? This could be a good opportunity to mentor them so that they enjoy what they do and thrive at it.

Be Reasonable

Presumably you are passionate about your business, but be reasonable. Everything can't be a fire drill with your team. Your employees like to work for someone who's passionate about what they do, but constant stress is good for no one. Make sure you are setting your team up for success by giving clear guidance, providing adequate resources, and maintaining a humility that allows them to feel comfortable coming to you to ask questions or make an additional suggestion.

Have a Positive Attitude

Every day isn't roses and red velvet cupcakes, but as the leader, it's your job to set aside your personal frustrations and focus on keeping the staff positive. If instead you take out your stress on them, you'll quickly lose their confidence and trust.

Give Yourself Time

Great leaders aren't born overnight. Instead, they are created over time. Like a hearty soup made over hours of cooking in a slow cooker, the experiences of a leader marry together over time to hone both leadership skills and leadership instincts and create a person who others want to follow.

Every time you meet a new challenge, you are becoming that leader. Even when you make a mistake, you are still becoming that leader. It may take time to replace poor habits with ones that will create a nurturing and collaborative environment in which you and everyone you work with can thrive. Give it time. You got this.

EMERSON'S action steps

1. Ask for feedback from your employees.
2. Schedule regular team meetings.
3. Be aware of how your leadership style is impacting your individual employees; you can tweak it accordingly.
4. Remember to cut yourself some slack. Great leaders are not born overnight; they develop through experience.

CHAPTER 20

Fifteen Things You Must Never Forget in Business

So you've started your business. Now what? This chapter is about the things that will keep you in business if you put them into practice.

If you take this chapter seriously and use what I preach here, you will shave years off of your learning curve as a new business owner. Trust me! This chapter focuses on understanding your profit model, timeliness, friendliness, paying attention, the concept that time is money, the importance of confirming the deal, and the importance of always looking for the next customer.

1. Make Sure You Know How Much Profit Is in Every Deal

Before you send pricing to any client, it is important to figure out what the job or contract is worth to you.

EMERSON'S essentials

If you don't have a background in accounting, make sure you get sound advice on your finances. You can learn some really expensive lessons if you do not understand profit margins up front. You can always reduce prices, run sales, and create promotional events to get customers in the door. But remember, you must cover your costs, or you will end up broke and out of business.

What are some of the things you need to consider in determining your profit? Let's say you run a tailoring business, for example. Here are some things to consider:

- **Cost of materials:** If you make suits or dresses, track the expense of fabric, buttons, thread, and trim for each garment you make.
- **Cost of labor:** If you are doing the work yourself, what is your time worth? $10/hour? $20/hour? $75/hour or more? Are you designing the garment yourself, or is the customer giving you the specifications? If you are paying an employee or freelancer to do the work, how much time will it take for him or her to make the garment? Your time is your money.
- **Overhead:** Businesses use many things that are not free—electricity, heat, rent, insurance, water, business licenses, advertising, legal fees, security, accounting costs, computers, software, cash registers, and office supplies. Some things are occasional expenses; others are weekly or monthly. All of them must be paid for by your business and should be reflected in your price. You should know how much

money it costs you to run your business each month, which is also known as your monthly burn rate.

EMERSON'S experience

Early on in my business, I had a one-size-fits-all pricing model. When I started analyzing my profits, I realized I was lucky if I made 25 percent gross revenue on any project. I still had to pay all overhead and taxes from that before I pocketed any money. This system got me nowhere fast.

Once I figured out that I wasn't making enough money on my projects, I sat down with my accountant and created a spreadsheet that told me exactly how much each job was costing me. My accountant also formatted my accounting software to track project expenses. I began to see how much profit there was in every project.

The costing breakdown forced me to justify my pricing, rather than determining pricing by using "gut" feelings or what I thought the customer would pay.

2. Qualify Prospects

As an entrepreneur, your time is the most valuable thing that you can give anyone. Qualify prospects before you agree to meet with them. If the client does not yet have a budget, perhaps he is not ready to buy. Conduct as much prework over the phone as possible and develop a checklist of things you need from the client prior to developing a quote or attending a meeting. If you can, offer to host the meeting in your office, so that you lose less time if he doesn't show up.

EMERSON'S essentials

Confirm appointments a day in advance. You can do this via technology or a live assistant, but make sure people know you are on their schedule to meet. When I schedule an appointment, I always get the cell number of the person with whom I am meeting. If I'm lost or might possibly be late, I can make a courtesy call.

3. Pay Attention to Marketing Trends

Things are changing with SEO, social media, mobile/web and text marketing, artificial intelligence, voice search, and online ads, and you could easily be left behind if you don't pay attention to changes in the marketplace. Make sure your website is updated every eighteen to twenty-four months. It must load quickly on any device. Take note of new keywords, hashtags, content ideas, and online marketing tactics. Video converts better than anything on all platforms.

4. Use Your Accountant As a Business Advisor

Your tax preparer is not your accountant. If you only talk to an accountant at tax time you are doing your business a disservice. Use your accountant to make strategic plans for your business. Your accountant should help you develop your annual budget every fall, and advise you on tax planning. They can also help you determine the right time to seek funding. Don't just leverage this professional for taxes.

EMERSON'S experience

When the pandemic hit in 2020 and the government released the stimulus many business owners were in trouble. The paperwork needed for the Paycheck Protection Program (PPP) loans (largely a grant program) required EIN authorization, 941 payroll filing forms, and current taxes that many business owners struggled to produce. So out of thirty million small business owners in the US only 5.2 million qualified for the stimulus money. Many were trying to call their tax preparer for help, and often those people were not helpful because they didn't have an ongoing business relationship. Accountants are business advisors whom you should speak with monthly.

5. Keep Your Files Organized

When your files are well organized you can respond to business opportunities more quickly. Throughout the course of your business, you will be asked to produce your foundational documents, things like your articles of incorporation, fictitious name registration, IRS letter assigning your Employer Identification Number (EIN), a passport, and your personal and business taxes. You should scan these records or save them as PDFs when they are sent to you so that you can retrieve them quickly.

6. Be a Lifelong Learner

Success leaves clues everywhere. One of the secrets to business success is constantly reading books on business, leadership, and social media. Throughout the years of running a business, work on growing your business acumen and leadership skills. Get degrees in business administration and take courses on business planning, leadership, marketing, and negotiation.

There are lots of mini-courses designed for busy business owners; take advantage of them. Be sure to check out my online business courses too at https://succeedasyourownboss.com.

7. Never Let a Customer Down

When you make a mistake in business, you have to own it and fix it quickly, no matter the cost. You must never let a customer down. Mistakes will happen, but it's best to call the customer and inform them of the issue rather than wait for an angry phone call. Tell them about the issue and how you will resolve it. It's not about the mistake. It's about how you make good on the mistake.

8. Build Partnerships

You should look at your employees, customers, and competitors as partners. Collaboration is much better than competition. If you partner with a competitor, you can compete for a larger piece of business together. Employees who feel like partners will treat their role in your business much differently than a rank-and-file employee who is looking at the clock waiting for quitting time. You don't just want to sell products and services; you want to partner with customers to create solutions for them. Be willing to brainstorm with your customers so that you can figure out how to fulfill their future needs.

9. Protect Your Business Credit

Pay your vendors on time. If you have a line of credit, use it for short-term expenses only. Once your client pays you, repay the line back in full immediately. Don't treat your line of credit like a credit card, otherwise you won't have space available when you need cash. Try to anticipate things and borrow money before you need it. Keep your personal credit score as high as possible; everything still goes back to that. Pay your taxes and quarterly payments on time. Having a tax lien can keep you from getting larger contracts. Keep all taxes up-to-date.

10. Focus On High-Value Activities

As a business owner, you must make sure that you are not spending your time doing administrative tasks that should be outsourced. If your time is billable at $250/hour don't spend it doing $30/hour work.

Make a "top 5" list the night before—and tackle the list each morning. Try to complete the five things by 11 a.m., and anything after that is a bonus. Writing the task list the night before will keep you focused. The list can be anything from sending five follow-up emails to paying bills, scheduling a lunch meeting, or calling your child's teacher. Make your "must-do" list at the end of each day and get more done.

11. Respect Your Client's Time

If she says she has only twenty minutes, that is all the time you have. If you keep her forty-five minutes, you have guaranteed you will never get an opportunity to work with her. Stay focused on your desired outcome of the meeting and recap the next steps in writing.

12. Be Early for Appointments

You can waste your time, but not your client's time. Always leave thirty minutes early for a customer meeting. Check for traffic jams. Have an idea of what parking is available near your client's office. Check the weather, and allow time for the walk to the building without rushing.

EMERSON'S experience

Early on in my business I began to get a reputation for being late. Then one of my mentors said someone had mentioned my problem to her. I realized this reputation was spreading and could damage my business. Since then, I have been the first to arrive at any meeting I attend. The key to being a good business owner is to take good advice and respond immediately.

13. Prospect All the Time

Your number one job as a business owner is to sell. Make sure everyone in your circle knows what you do and has enough information to refer you to people. Read everything you can, including *The New York Times*, Bloomberg, *Inc.*, and your local business journal. You never know where you'll see a lead or just a good idea that you should incorporate into your business. Network online and offline; you never know who you are talking to and how they might be able to help you. Make sure you know everyone in your town that can loan your business money or provide business assistance. Take advantage of every opportunity possible to fill your pipeline.

14. There's No Such Thing As a Handshake Deal

Attorneys have a saying: "A conversation never happened until you confirm it in writing." There will be times in your business when you deal with clients who promise you things or tell you it's a deal, and then things fall apart. Do yourself a favor: Do not start any work or ship any product until you get a signed contract or purchase order.

Clients are sometimes subject to the internal politics of their companies. There's no such thing as a handshake deal or a verbal agreement. Get everything in writing. Always send an email after a meeting to clarify what was agreed to and any action steps.

15. Always Remember ABC

There are three things that you can control every day: Attitude, Behavior, and Commitment. No matter what happens, you need to always remember what you can control. People will disappoint you. Employees may make you angry. But you must always maintain control. Never respond in writing in anger; just take a few deep breaths, pick up the phone, and listen first to what the other party is trying to convey before you respond. Always show empathy even when you haven't received any kindness. Do good work and be good to work with. No one wants to work with a high-maintenance small business owner. That doesn't mean you take abuse from a client. Learn how to advocate for yourself in a way that doesn't destroy the relationship. Learn to say "I can't agree to that" with grace, and stay committed to your mission.

EMERSON'S experience

It's stressful to run a business, but the good days far outweigh the bad days. I look for ways to reduce my stress, such as running, yoga, salsa dancing, regular massages, bike riding, long baths, or learning to play golf. Be good to yourself. Resting is an activity. There are no awards for "most overworked business owner." Becoming a chronic workaholic is a great way to ruin your health and your personal life. Make sure you have a life outside of your business. Resist the urge to join #TeamNoSleep. Don't fool yourself into thinking you can maintain your edge without proper rest.

Be grateful for the journey. Be grateful for all the lessons, even the most expensive ones. Bad employees and clients will come and go. You'll just be better at avoiding these folks the next time. Trust your gut. If it doesn't feel good, don't do it. You must be brave to start a business, but you must keep pushing yourself to stay in business. What you have always done won't work forever, so be flexible. Your business should allow you to live your dream life. If not, you might need to pivot or reinvent your business. But that is okay, because you'll be smarter about things the next time.

By the way, I have a special gift for you for reading this far. I have some bonus chapters to give you from previous versions of this book that will help you get to the top even faster. To download the material, head over to https://succeedasyourownboss.com/bookbonus.

CHAPTER 21

FINAL THOUGHTS

After You Start

Today you should start thinking of your job as a temporary situation. Do what you have to do, so you can do what you want to do. You now have a road map for business success. Plan your life, then plan your dream business.

You now know what it takes to develop a life plan, financially reposition yourself, solidify your business idea, develop the marketing strategy, and then write the business plan. Key to all of your entrepreneurial dreams coming true will be your ability to manage your finances and save. Start cutting back on your expenses today. Use a budget and engage your whole family in its development. Make sure your spouse or family is behind you. Plan for all the insurance you will need (health, life, disability).

Be very discreet about your business plans. Use the five-finger rule: Don't tell more than five people about your idea, including your momma. Be honest with yourself about what skills you have and what skills you will need to run your business. Think about who you are going to need to help you be successful in your business. Find a small business development center in your area and make an appointment. Start thinking about your marketing strategy and your business plan. Remember, your business plan is a living, breathing document that should be reviewed and updated every two months in the first couple of years you're in business to make sure your business is on the right track.

Work Your Network

You need to become a networking machine. Make new friends and use this planning year to reconnect with old contacts. People do business with people they like, know, and trust. Hone your selling skills by joining small business organizations and networking groups to put yourself out there.

The key to effective networking is building a genuine relationship. First, look for ways to give. Then promote your product or service when asked. The bedrock of entrepreneurship is word-of-mouth referrals. If people not only like you but also believe in what you are selling, you have a valuable marketing tool that will keep on generating business for you.

Remember the Seven Essential Principles of Small Business Success

Success leaves clues everywhere. Business owners who survive in business over the long haul have some common traits. They are relentlessly persistent, positive, patient, committed, and resilient. They have sales systems and follow-up systems, and they understand their customers' needs and wants intimately. Here are the Seven Essential Principles of Small Business Success:

1. Have an entrepreneurial mindset.
2. Observe strict fiscal discipline.
3. Utilize a kitchen cabinet of advisors.
4. Have a defined brand.
5. Focus on a niche market.
6. Provide excellent customer service.
7. Carefully manage your banking relationship.

Claim Success from the Beginning

If you do not believe in your success, no one else will. Before you do anything in your business, tell people about the great results you're expecting to achieve. Some people may be naysayers, but stay focused on the end result. Find a quote, phrase, or Bible verse that inspires you. Print it out and tape it to the wall. On hard days, read it out loud to push away doubt.

Grow Yourself to Grow Your Business

Make yourself a student of small business. You need to learn all you can about the business of running a business in order to be successful. There is a whole business world out there that you do not know enough about yet. You will have some tough days ahead. Business ownership is not easy. If it were, one out of three business owners would not fail in their second year of operation. Like my father used to say, "You wouldn't know good days, if it wasn't for bad days." Savor all your good days and the hard-learned lessons in your business.

Get Yourself a Personal Theme Song

Pick a song that always makes you feel good and gives you energy. Play your song anytime you need an attitude adjustment or a confidence boost.

Make the Difference Clear

Take time to develop your signature move. Determine your value proposition. What will be your competitive advantage? What is your niche? How will you compete? Will you be cheaper, better, faster, or a one-stop option? With limited time and resources, the narrower your target focus the easier it will be to plan your marketing efforts. Remember, your mindset can hold you back.

Set SMART Goals

A goal is nothing more than a dream with a deadline. Remember to set Specific, Measurable, Attainable, Realistic, and Timely goals. Make a timeline for your process, and give yourself milestones to hit.

The key to realizing your dreams is organizing your time. Give your business venture two hours a day for starters. Stop watching TV, and go to bed earlier to find the time.

Seven Things to Measure

Many small business owners work in their businesses and not on them. Make sure you are measuring the performance of all aspects of your business operations. Here is what you should be focusing on in your small business:

1. **Measure your marketing.** When you put together a marketing plan for your business, be sure that you're tracking your return

on investment. If the tactics that you're using—email, coupons, direct mail, social media, online ads—aren't providing a return, then don't continue to waste money on them.

2. **Measure your profit margin on every sale.** If your business is not making a profit you won't be in business for long. Watch your profit margins on every sale to make sure that you have a sustainable difference between the cost to make and deliver your products or services and the price that you actually charge the customer. If there is no profit, adjust your price or reduce the cost of goods to increase the margin.

3. **Monitor your cash flow closely.** Track your cash flow weekly and monthly, so you know what's coming in and what's going out. Use accounting software to make the process easier. Ask your accountant to teach you to read financial statements.

4. **Measure your website traffic.** Use Google Analytics to measure the unique visitors stopping by your website monthly. Once you know the content that captures their attention, produce more of it. Pay close attention to which social platforms are sending referral traffic. It doesn't matter whether you're an online or brick-and-mortar business, your website is your best sales tool.

5. **Grow your email list.** Your email list is an asset and a license to sell. Always grow your list. Use content, ebooks, webinars, and online ads to drive traffic to your landing pages to build your list. Provide valuable information to your customers and they won't leave you.

6. **Watch your overhead expenses.** Overhead costs sink a lot of small businesses. Expenses like payroll, rent, bank fees and interest, shipping, software subscriptions, equipment leases, and phone bills should be closely tracked and measured.

7. **Measure your sales.** Track your sales on a weekly basis. Pay attention to your sales cycles. You'll notice trends that will help you know when to do more marketing to generate revenue in the business.

Use up-to-date financial information to make business decisions. Be an informed business owner, by testing and measuring everything.

Save for Retirement!

Once you start generating an income from your business and earning a regular paycheck, save for retirement! Consider placing a percentage of your business income in a profit account or a SEP IRA or Solo 401(k) or other small business retirement account. SEP and 401(k) accounts are easy to set up, and your contributions are tax deductible. Once your accounts are established, you can contribute every year up to your tax filing deadline, including any extensions. Your contributions can vary each year, offering you some flexibility when the business has a down year.

I wrote this book because I wanted to share everything I have learned as a small business owner. I love entrepreneurs. You are tireless and the bravest people on the planet. You are the idea person with the big vision. The world needs you to survive. You create jobs, provide benefits for your employees, and provide the highest quality of service to your customers. Being a small business owner is a spiritual journey; you will be stretched in ways that you cannot imagine. The best thing you can do for your business is pray over it every day, and remember God's Promise. And if you ever find your business in a rut, reread this book, examine your business profile at https://smallbizlady.lpages.co/bossquiz/, and check out the latest courses at www.smallbizladyuniversity.com. I will get you back on track.

Here is my best advice for small business success:

You never lose in business. Either you WIN or you LEARN! If I have helped you, please email me at melinda@melindaemerson.com and tell me your story. I love to hear from dedicated entrepreneurs.

Be flexible. Stay positive and coachable. I wish you the very best.

SAMPLE CUSTOMER SATISFACTION SURVEY

Here's a sample customer service survey you can use to understand your customer's experience with your business.

We thank you for your business. Please provide us your feedback on a scale from 1 to 5 using this criteria:

1 = Poor 2 = Fair 3 = Good 4 = Very Good 5 = Excellent

❏ Did you have a good shopping experience? _____
❏ Was the staff courteous and helpful? _____
❏ Did you find everything you needed? _____
❏ Did you receive good value for the price? _____
❏ What could have improved your buying experience? _____
❏ Would you do business with us again? _____
❏ Would you refer us to a friend or colleague? _____
❏ Do you have any additional feedback? _____

_____

_____

_____

May we contact you for additional comments?

❏ Yes
❏ No
❏ Name _____
❏ Phone/email _____

Further Resources

Books

Here's a list of what I consider to be the essential business books that every small business owner should read. From marketing to profit and everything in between, these are business books that should be on your shelf if you want to study to up your game.

Carder, Susie, *Power Your Profits: How to Take Your Business from $10,000 to $10,000,000*. Atria Books, 2020.

Carnegie, Dale, *How to Win Friends & Influence People*. Simon & Schuster, 2009.

Chandler, Stephanie, *Own Your Niche: Hype-Free Internet Marketing Tactics to Establish Authority in Your Field and Promote Your Service-Based Business*. Authority Publishing, 2012.

Delaney, Laurel J., *Exporting: The Definitive Guide to Selling Abroad Profitably*. Apress, 2013.

Emerson, Melinda, *Fix Your Business: A 90-Day Plan to Get Back Your Life and Reduce Chaos in Your Business*. Authority Publishing, 2018.

Fotopulos, Dawn, *Accounting for the Numberphobic: A Survival Guide for Small Business Owners*. AMACOM, 2014.

Gerber, Michael E., *The E-Myth Revisited: Why Most Small Businesses Don't Work and What to Do About It*. Harper Business, 2004.

Khalfani-Cox, Lynnette, *Zero Debt: The Ultimate Guide to Financial Freedom (3rd ed.)*. Advantage World Press, 2016.

Michalowicz, Mike, *Profit First: Transform Your Business from a Cash-Eating Monster to a Money-Making Machine*. Portfolio, 2017.

Meerman Scott, David, *The New Rules of Marketing and PR: How to Use Content Marketing, Podcasting, Social Media, AI, Live Video, and Newsjacking to Reach Buyers Directly (7th ed.)*. Wiley, 2020.

Miller, Donald, *Building a StoryBrand: Clarify Your Message So Customers Will Listen*. HarperCollins Leadership, 2017.

Samit, Jay, *Disrupt You!: Master Personal Transformation, Seize Opportunity, and Thrive in the Era of Endless Innovation.* Flatiron Books, 2015.

Whatley, Tony, *SideHustle Millionaire: How to Build a Side Business That Creates Financial Freedom.* Independently Published, 2018.

If you buy business books and never get around to reading them, consider subscribing to Soundview Executive Book Summaries, www.summary.com. This company provides concise summaries of recently published business books.

Government Documents

US Census Bureau
The Census Bureau serves as the leading source of quality data about the nation's people and economy.
www.census.gov

US Copyright Office
101 Independence Avenue SE
Washington, DC 20559–6000
1-202-707-3000
www.copyright.gov

US Department of Labor
The Department of Labor promotes the welfare of the job seekers, wage earners, and retirees of the United States. They also track changes in employment and prices, and other national economic measurements.
www.dol.gov

International Trade Administration
A federal resource for information about markets and industries throughout the world.
www.trade.gov

System for Award Management
The federal government's marketplace for all federal contracts.
www.sam.gov

Internal Revenue Service
The IRS has a Small Business and Self-Employed Tax Center.
www.irs.gov/businesses/small

Minority Business Development Agency (MBDA)
This agency, part of the US Department of Commerce, was created to foster the establishment and growth of minority-owned businesses in America.
www.mbda.gov

Office of the National Ombudsman (SBA program)
The National Ombudsman's primary mission is to assist small businesses when they experience excessive or unfair federal regulatory enforcement actions.
www.sba.gov/ombudsman

Occupational Safety and Health Administration (OSHA)
This agency outlines and administers specific health and safety standards employers must provide for the protection of employees.
www.osha.gov

US Small Business Administration (SBA)
The Small Business Administration provides information and resources that will help you at any stage of the business lifecycle.
www.sba.gov

SCORE (Service Corps of Retired Executives)
This is the best source of free and confidential small business advice to help you build your business.
www.score.org

Small Business Development Center National Information Clearinghouse
The SBDCNet serves as a resource providing timely, relevant research, web-based information, and training to SBDC counselors and their small business clients.
www.sbdcnet.org

US Patent and Trademark Office
This office administers all issues having to do with patents and trademarks.
Email TrademarkAssistanceCenter@ uspto.gov.
www.uspto.gov

Women-Owned Small Businesses Program
This site is the gateway for women-owned businesses selling to the federal government.
www.sba.gov/content/ women-owned-small-business-program

For a more extensive list of web resources available to the aspiring small business owner, visit my website at https://succeedasyourownboss.com or www.smallbizladyuniversity.com.

INDEX

About the Author

Melinda Emerson, MBA, the "SmallBizLady," is America's number one small business expert. She is an internationally renowned keynote speaker on small business, social media, and content marketing. Melinda is CEO of Quintessence Group, her marketing consulting firm, which serves *Fortune* 500 brands that target the small business market. In addition to being a former *New York Times* columnist, she is frequently quoted by media organizations including *The Wall Street Journal, Forbes*, MSNBC, CNBC, ABC News, and Black Enterprise. She is the host of the *SmallBizChat* podcast, and publishes a resource blog, SucceedAsYourOwnBoss.com. Her advice is widely read, reaching three million entrepreneurs each week online. She is a graduate of Virginia Tech, and holds an MBA from Drexel University. She resides in Drexel Hill, Pennsylvania.